Georgia's Historic Restaurants and Their Recipes

OTHER TITLES IN JOHN F. BLAIR'S *HISTORIC RESTAURANTS* SERIES™

Arizona's Historic Restaurants and Their Recipes
by Karen Surina Mulford

Florida's Historic Restaurants and Their Recipes
by Dawn O'Brien and Becky Roper Matkov

Maryland's Historic Restaurants and Their Recipes
by Dawn O'Brien and Rebecca Schenck

North Carolina's Historic Restaurants and Their Recipes
by Dawn O'Brien

Pennsylvania's Historic Restaurants and Their Recipes
by Dawn O'Brien and Claire Walter

South Carolina's Historic Restaurants and Their Recipes
by Dawn O'Brien and Karen Mulford

Virginia's Historic Restaurants and Their Recipes
by Dawn O'Brien

Georgia's Historic Restaurants and Their Recipes

by
Dawn O'Brien
and
Jean Spaugh

Drawings by

Debra Long Hampton

and Patsy Faires

John F. Blair, Publisher
Winston-Salem, North Carolina

Second Edition

Original edition © 1987

DESIGN BY DEBRA LONG HAMPTON

MAP BY DEBRA LONG HAMPTON

JACKET PHOTOGRAPHS BY BERNARD CARPENTER

PRINTED AND BOUND BY R. R. DONNELLEY & SONS

Library of Congress Cataloging-in-Publication Data

O'Brien, Dawn.

Georgia's historic restaurants and their recipes / by Dawn O'Brien
and Jean Spaugh. — 2nd ed.

p.   cm.

Reprint. Originally published: Winston-Salem, N.C. : J. F. Blair, 1987.

Includes index.

ISBN 0-89587-157-2 (alk. paper)

1. Cookery, American — Southern style. 2. Cookery — Georgia.
3. Restaurants — Georgia — Guidebooks. 4. Historic buildings — Georgia.

I. Spaugh, Jean. II. Title.

TX715.2.S68027   1997

641.59758 — dc20   96-43723

Dedication

I would like to dedicate my part of this book to my best friend, Betty Jo Gilley. B. J., like a firefly, lit up the darkness with her magic.

Dawn O'Brien

I'd like to thank sweet Richard Spaugh, whom I am nominating for sainthood.

Jean Spaugh

Contents

Foreword

All of us have some special interest that sparks a gleam in our eye, some subject we can wax eloquent on — or at least wish we had the words to do it justice. For me, that special thing is historic restaurants that serve good food.

When it became apparent, after researching and writing two books on the subject, that I needed collaborators for the books that would follow, I knew exactly what sort of person I needed. I had to find someone for each book who would feel the elation I experience when discovering a historic restaurant. I needed someone who, after biting into a sweet, ripe piece of fruit, would roll the flavor about the tongue, trying to capture the particular essence of the fruit *so she or he could describe it to someone else*. In other words, I needed a writer. I have been lucky to find collaborators who not only share my passion concerning history and cuisine but who can write also.

My collaborator for this book was Jean Spaugh. By the time we were midway through our travels in Georgia, Jean was amazed at the incredible variety of historic restaurants and the heterogeneous mix of cuisines we found. Take the terms *continental* and *down-home cooking*. They vary not only from state to state but also from region to region within the same state. Each restaurant has its own brand of cuisine, but more than that, each has its own architecture, history, and amusing stories to tell. Those differences are a big part of why it has been so much fun to follow *North Carolina's Historic Restaurants and Their Recipes* with books on numerous other states.

For those of you not familiar with any of the other books in this series, let me explain the criteria Jean and I used in our selection of restaurants. Generally, the building housing the restaurant had to be at least fifty years old, or had to be reconstructed of materials more than fifty years old on a historically significant site. Our criteria are less rigorous and complex than those of the National Register of Historic Buildings, but we follow the same basic approach to what defines a historic building.

The other standards we use have to do with the food, atmosphere, and service, and we readily admit that these factors can be subjective. If one of your favorite historic restaurants in Georgia is not in this book, there could be many reasons for the omission. We had to limit the number to fifty; some restaurants weren't interested in participating; others didn't want to divulge their recipes. And, occasionally, we received recipes that we couldn't get to come out right even after we'd tested them several times. After all, our book is basically for home cooks, and if we can't make a dish taste as it did in the restaurant, we don't want you to waste your time on it either.

Georgia's historic restaurants make good memories. Whenever and wherever you are traveling in Georgia, call ahead to check serving hours, then take every opportunity to visit these delightful places. And when you can't go yourself, just make one of the scrumptious recipes in your own kitchen. If your family is anything like Jean's or mine, they'll love tasting new and unusual dishes. Jean's family now regularly demands The Rankin Quarter's Banana Fluff. And my husband keeps asking when I'm going to make LaPrade's Cabbage in Cheese Sauce again. I bet you'll discover many dishes that will become a tradition in your own home. *Bon appétit*! Or, as my children would say, "Chow down!"

Acknowledgments

G eorgia is a beautiful state that overflows with caring people. They care about their heritage and work to see that it is preserved. And, in our case, we found that a surprising number of people were willing to share their knowledge and experiences with us. We received help not only from the expected places, but also from many unexpected sources. We are grateful for the help of so many people, but would particularly like to thank those who follow.

To: The restaurateurs and chefs who gave us good stories, good food, and good recipes.

To: Barbara Daniels at the Tourist Division of the Georgia Department of Industry and Trade, and to tourism representatives Becky Aliff, Becky Bassett, Jeannie Buttrum, Mary Jo Dudley, Kitty Peoples, Kitty Sikes, Cheryl Smith, Carol Spires, Ruth Sykes, and Dawn Townsend.

To: Jenny Stacy of the Savannah Convention and Visitors Bureau.

To: Sheryl Johnson of the Georgia Visitors Center.

To: The artists Debbie Hampton and Patsy Faires for translating photos into works of art.

To: Ronnie Thomas, who crisscrossed Georgia faithfully scanning the map and saying, "I think we should have turned back there."

To: Jeannette Christopher, teacher of history and cooking, who still corrects bad grammar.

To: Saxton Powell and Betty Jo Gilley for helping with the testing and retesting of recipes.

To: The guinea-pig recipe tasters who stroked our and the chefs' egos with their effusive compliments and instructional criticisms.

To: Jane Brock for keeping this book on the right path through Georgia.

Georgia

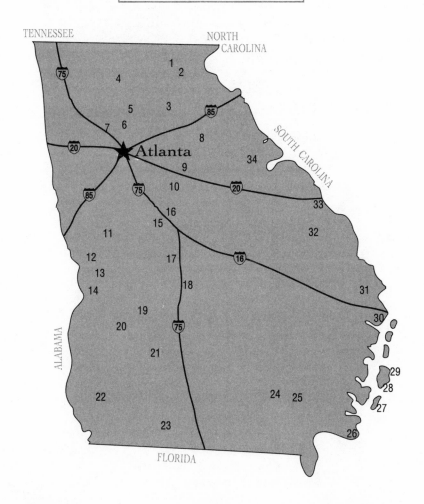

The Stovall House

1526 Ga. 255 North
(5 miles east of Helen off Ga.17)
SAUTEE

People were on the veranda attentively listening to a storyteller as I approached the old white clapboard house on a clear summer day. As I stopped for a while to enjoy the story, the rich aroma of dinner drifted out the open windows.

Inside the stunningly renovated home, the highly polished floors and Schwartz family antiques make you feel at home.

Seated for dinner on an enclosed porch with a good view of Lynch Mountain, I noticed a child's swing hanging from a massive tree. I thought once again of the storyteller's tale of the house and grounds. The land was once owned by the Cherokees, who were driven off by white settlers. The settlers drew lots for the land, and Moses Harshaw, reputed to have been the meanest man who ever lived, drew this parcel. He built his home here in 1837, using locally harvested black walnut trees to make the doors and fireplace mantels. In addition to throwing his slaves off Lynch Mountain when they were no longer of use to him, he supposedly demanded that his young daughter, who had died when he was away, be exhumed so he could examine the expensive dress his wife had purchased for her burial. Watching a butterfly land on the swing, I decided that the epitaph on Harshaw's tombstone was most fitting: "He is dead and gone to hell."

In the late 1800s, the Stovalls bought the house. Then, in order to attract a doctor to northern Georgia, the house was offered to Dr. Walter, who was later much beloved for opening his home to the public. That tradition has continued under the proprietorship of the Schwartz family, who renovated the attic into lovely bedrooms with baths.

Although the pleasant location and the relaxed atmosphere under owner Hamilton "Ham" Schwartz enhance a visit to The Stovall House, the best part is the creative cuisine. The restaurant's Ham and Cheddar Phyllo was hearty, light, and especially delicious. Because a man nearby raved about his Stuffed Chicken, filled with cream cheese and herbs, I couldn't resist sampling that dish, too; I knew immediately that readers would want to know about this scrumptious creation.

Would I neglect dessert in a place like this? No way! And you shouldn't either, especially if the restaurant is serving its wonderful Chocolate Orange Pie.

The Stovall House's Chocolate Orange Pie

³/4 cup sugar
¹/4 cup cocoa
¹/4 cup milk
¹/8 teaspoon cream of tartar
2 8-ounce packages cream cheese, softened

¹/8 cup whipping cream
1¹/2 teaspoons orange liqueur
zest from ¹/4 orange
graham cracker pie shell

In a small saucepan, combine sugar, cocoa, milk, and cream of tartar. Cook over medium heat until mixture is a soft ball. Set aside. In a large mixing bowl, combine cream cheese, whipping cream, orange liqueur, and orange zest. Blend until creamy and smooth. Add fudge mixture and blend until well mixed. Pour into pie shell and chill several hours until set. Yields 1 pie.

The Stovall House's Stuffed Chicken

8 ounces cream cheese
1 teaspoon basil
1 teaspoon chives
1 teaspoon dill
1 clove garlic, crushed
8 boneless chicken breasts, halved

vegetable oil
flour for dredging
2 eggs, beaten
1 cup breadcrumbs

Let cream cheese soften to room temperature. In a small bowl, mix cream cheese with herbs and garlic. Flatten chicken breasts and roll each breast around a walnut-size dollop of herb cheese. Cover and chill for at least 1 hour. Put ¼ inch of oil in a skillet and heat to medium. Place flour, eggs, and breadcrumbs in separate bowls. Dredge chicken in flour, then egg, then breadcrumbs. Sauté chicken until lightly browned on all sides. Place chicken on a greased baking sheet and bake at 350 degrees for 30 minutes. Serves 8.

The Stovall House's Ham and Cheddar Phyllo

2 tablespoons butter
1 cup all-purpose flour
1 cup milk
2 cups grated cheddar cheese
4 cups cooked ham

2 cups broccoli
dash of pepper
dash of cayenne
8 sheets phyllo
$^1/_3$ to $^1/_2$ cup melted butter

In a large skillet, melt 2 tablespoons butter and add flour. Stir into a smooth roux. Slowly add milk, stirring until well incorporated. Add cheese, ham, broccoli, and seasonings. Stir until cheese melts and flavors combine.

Lay 1 sheet of phyllo on a lightly floured surface. Brush with melted butter. Lay second layer over the first. Place about ¼ of filling at center of phyllo. Fold phyllo into thirds as you would fold a letter and seal with butter. Repeat procedure until all filling is used. Place phyllo pastries on greased cookie sheet, brush top of each phyllo with butter, and cook in a 350-degree oven for 10 minutes. Slice while hot and serve. Serves 6 to 8.

Nacoochee Valley Guest House
Bed-and-Breakfast Inn

2220 Ga. 17
SAUTEE

If you are an overnight guest who arrives during blueberry season, expect to be handed a bucket for harvesting the berries in owner Bernadette "Bernie" Yates's backyard. *Casual* and *homespun* take on entirely new meanings at this country French inn, even if you're only stopping for lunch.

Chickasaw Indians have lived in this region since 10,000 B.C., when the Nacoochee Valley was named after a Cherokee chief's daughter. Nacoochee fell in love with Sautee, a Chickasaw brave, at the crossroads where the Old Sautee Store now stands. The lovers tried to make peace between the warring tribes but met tragic deaths at nearby Yonah Mountain. You can't see Yonah from the inn's enclosed back-porch bay window, but you can see the purple peaks of Lynch Mountain.

It was a crisp February day when I found my way to the home built in 1920 for the Crumley family. Each of the inn's dining rooms is different, but the fire burning in the Rose Dining Room settled my choice. Print tablecloths overlaid with lace were set with part of Bernie's collection of salt and pepper shakers and napkin rings. Your table may be set with sterling silver offset by a vase of fresh flowers. When I admired a set of 1849 hand-painted Limoges plates hanging on the wall, I learned that Bernie had bought them by saving quarters from her waitress days.

The menu — French with continental overtones — is as spontaneous and irrepressible as the hostess herself. Because Bernie doesn't like to waste kitchen time, she makes a quick, delicious bread with a texture so light that it's almost like cake. I began with a knockout French Onion Soup. When I couldn't decide between her Salad Niçoise and Caesar Salad with Shrimp, I ended up sampling both. When Bernie learned that I was open to new tastes, she added scallops to the Caesar, which changed the taste altogether. But her *pièce de résistance* was a Chocolate Hazelnut Bombe sitting on a cloud of billowy Chantilly Cream.

Lunch
11:30 A.M. until 2:00 P.M.
Monday through Saturday

Dinner
6:00 P.M. until 8:30 P.M.
Wednesday through Saturday

For reservations
(suggested)
call (706) 878-3830

Among the building's many occupants was a stress clinic. In a way, the inn still serves that function, because a wonderful meal and a night at this serendipitous hideaway could erase any stress you brought along.

Nacoochee Valley's Caesar Salad with Scallops and Shrimp

¼ cup cider vinegar
1 egg
3 or 4 anchovies
juice of ½ lemon
3 or 4 large cloves garlic
1 teaspoon Dijon mustard
3 dashes Worcestershire sauce
1 cup olive oil

10 large sea scallops
10 large shrimp,
    peeled and deveined
salt and pepper to taste
1 head romaine lettuce
½ cup Parmesan cheese, grated
1 cup seasoned croutons

In a food processor, combine vinegar, egg, anchovies, lemon juice, 2 cloves garlic, Dijon, and Worcestershire. Pulse to blend mixture. With motor running, slowly add all but 3 tablespoons of oil. Heat remaining oil in a sauté pan; chop remaining garlic and heat in oil, stirring until garlic begins to soften. Add scallops and shrimp and sauté until shrimp are pink and scallops are done. Add salt and pepper. Place torn lettuce in each of 4 medium bowls and add scallops, shrimp, and cheese. Pour only enough dressing to lightly coat mixture and toss to combine. Add croutons and serve. Serves 4.

Nacoochee Valley's Beer Bread

3 cups self-rising flour
¹/₃ cup sugar
12-ounce bottle of beer

1 teaspoon dill seed
1 tablespoon sesame seed

Combine first 4 ingredients and pour into a 9-by-5-inch greased and floured loaf pan. Sprinkle top with sesame seeds and bake in a preheated 350-degree oven for 30 to 40 minutes. Yields a 1-pound loaf.

Pie

12 ounces semisweet
 chocolate chips
6 tablespoons butter
3 rounded teaspoons cocoa
1 teaspoon hazelnut liqueur

½ cup sugar
5 eggs, separated
½ cup ground walnuts
8-inch chocolate piecrust
 (homemade or commercial)

In a double boiler, melt chocolate, butter, cocoa, and liqueur. Transfer to an electric mixer and blend in sugar. Add yolks 1 at a time until sugar is dissolved and thickened. In a separate bowl, beat egg whites until stiff. Fold whites *carefully* into chocolate mixture. Sprinkle walnuts in bottom of piecrust and pour mixture into crust. Cover tightly with 2 layers aluminum foil and put in freezer overnight.

Chantilly Cream

1 cup whipping cream
2 tablespoons confectioners' sugar
1 teaspoon apricot brandy
 or lemon extract

1 egg white, stiffly beaten

In an electric mixer, whip cream until stiff peaks form. Add sugar 1 tablespoon at a time. Add brandy or lemon extract a little at a time. Fold in egg white and combine thoroughly.

To serve, pipe Chantilly Cream in a circle on each plate. Set a slice of unthawed Chocolate Hazelnut Bombe in center. Yields 8 to 10 servings.

LaPrade's

Route 1, Ga. 197 North, 18 miles from Clarkesville
CLARKESVILLE

*F*isherman on Lake Burton and hunters in the Appalachian Mountains know what the tolling of the bell means at LaPrade's. It announces mealtime! On the morning of my visit, the melodious announcement came at 7:45, and it meant that the long, handmade dining tables, covered with practical white vinyl, were about to be laden with an eye-opening country breakfast.

The sun was just breaking through the mountain fog as I sat down beside a flock of hungry people in the wood-paneled dining room. We were served family-style. Huge platters of Country Ham and Sausage were brought to our table first. These were immediately followed by bowls of Red-Eye Gravy, Grits, and Scrambled Eggs and plates of hot Biscuits. Sorghum syrup, honey, and jellies were eagerly passed as our cups were continually filled with steaming coffee.

I tried several different combinations, ladling Red-Eye Gravy on my Grits and topping my Biscuits with butter and honey. And like my table mates, I rarely let a full plate pass without trying a little bit more Country Ham or Sausage. While we devoured our hearty meal, my friendly neighbors chatted with me. I learned that many had come here as children.

The old fish camp affectionately known as LaPrade's began around the turn of the century when John LaPrade bought six hundred acres of land near the town of Burton, which was located in what is now the area north of Burton Island. Back in 1916, the lake was built to harness the Tallulah River as a power supply. At that time, John LaPrade built a camp to house and feed the lake's engineers and workers, but after the completion of the lake in 1925, the camp was opened to the public as a fishing retreat. Since then, generations of

12

families have come to stay in the little cabins and dine three times a day in the mountain tradition of garden vegetables, Fried Chicken, Cornbread, and old-fashioned desserts.

After breakfast, many guests hurried to get out on the well-stocked lake, but there were a few, like me, who chose to sit out on the porch in the old wooden rockers. One guest told a story of catching a striped bass, a fish (he explained) that is able to eat half its weight each day. Another guest joined in: "That's not so hard to believe. I just got through doing that in the dining room." I knew exactly what he meant.

LaPrade's Baked Apples

12 medium, tart apples
1½ cups sugar
1 teaspoon cinnamon
1 teaspoon nutmeg
1 teaspoon allspice
1 stick butter

Core and quarter apples and place in a large, greased baking dish. Mix sugar and spices together and sprinkle evenly over apples. Slice butter in ¼-inch wedges and place evenly over apples. Bake in a preheated 375-degree oven for 45 to 60 minutes until apples are soft. Serves 6.

LaPrade's Cabbage in Cheese Sauce

1 large head of cabbage
1 teaspoon salt
3 tablespoons butter
2 tablespoons sifted
  all-purpose flour
1 cup milk
2 cups grated American cheese
1 cup buttered breadcrumbs

Core and quarter cabbage and place in a saucepan with salted water. Cover and cook for 10 minutes until tender. Drain water and place cabbage in a greased casserole dish. Melt butter in a skillet and stir in flour until mixture is smooth. Add milk and cook over medium heat, stirring constantly until sauce is smooth and thickened. Add cheese and stir until melted. Pour sauce over cabbage and cover evenly with breadcrumbs. Bake in a preheated 350-degree oven for 20 minutes until breadcrumbs are brown. Serves 6.

LaPrade's Potato Patties

6 medium Kennebec potatoes
1 tablespoon salt
½ tablespoon black pepper
3 ounces all-purpose flour
¼ cup evaporated milk
1 egg

½ stick butter
½ medium Vidalia onion, chopped
1 mild or hot pepper, chopped
   (optional)
oil

Peel and quarter potatoes and place them in a pot with enough salted water to cover. Cook until tender, then drain. Place potatoes in a mixing bowl and mash with pepper, flour, milk, egg, butter, and onion. When well mixed, add mild or hot pepper if desired and shape mixture into patties. Place patties in a large, oiled iron frying pan. Bake in a preheated 350-degree oven until patties are golden brown on each side. Drain on paper towels. Yields 12 patties.

Glen-Ella Springs Inn

Route 3 (Bear Gap Road) near Clarkesville
CLARKESVILLE

A hundred years ago in Georgia, everybody who could afford it went to the mountains for the summer to escape the yellow fever and malaria which consumed the rest of the state. A good many of them traveled by train. They would be met at the Tallulah Falls station by a horse and buggy and transported into the mountains and past Tallulah Falls, a spectacular waterfall that wrapped visitors in a droning roar and drowned out all their cares.

Many stayed at Glen-Ella Springs Inn, a charming two-story pine hotel with wide

May 30 through October 31 —
Dinner
6:00 P.M. until 9:30 P.M.
Daily

Remainder of the Year —
Dinner
6:00 P.M. until 8:30 P.M.
Sunday through Thursday

6:00 P.M. until 9:30 P.M.
Friday and Saturday

For reservations
(necessary)
call (706) 754-7295

porches and a healing spring run by—you guessed it—a couple named Glen and Ella, the Davidsons. Here, weary guests would rest, feast on home-cooked food grown right on the family farm, and take invigorating hikes. A few hardy souls hiked into the gorge where the waterfall raged.

Then came progress. Tallulah Falls was dammed by the Corps of Engineers. No more water, no more roar, no more tourists. Air conditioning allowed people to stay in the city and work for fifty weeks a year. Fast food enabled them to work through lunch and dinner, too.

Then more progress. People reinvented weekends under the guise of "getting out of town." They reinvented hikes, calling them aerobic exercise, reinvented fresh food, calling it—well, fresh food. Glen-Ella Springs Inn reopened.

It has a hunting-lodge feeling now—a stone fireplace, Windsor chairs, plaid tablecloths. The floors are yellow pine, the walls accented with prints of nearby historical sites. The food is decidedly not country, or at least not fried-chicken country. It is more fried-Brie country. When I had dinner here, everything was so pretty I felt like taking a picture of my plate. The menu features dishes like Muscovy Duck Breast, Charleston Low Country Shrimp and Gravy, and my personal favorite, Honey-Roasted Rack of Lamb with Horse-radish-Mint Sauce. I got the lamb recipe, along with one for Apple Bread Pudding with Cinnamon Ice Cream.

It is possible to sleep here, too—Glen-Ella Springs Inn has sixteen rooms, a swimming pool, seventeen acres of meadow, and a creek. The train is gone, and Tallulah Falls is gone, but you can still comfort yourself with a swim and a hike and have another helping of Apple Bread Pudding to drown out all your cares.

Glen-Ella Springs Inn's Honey-Roasted Rack of Lamb with Horseradish-Mint Sauce

Horseradish-Mint Sauce

16 ounces apple-mint jelly
1 tablespoon horseradish

1 tablespoon cider vinegar
1 tablespoon fresh mint, chopped

In a saucepan, heat jelly until melted and stir in horseradish and vinegar. Let cool. Stir in chopped mint. Sauce will keep 1 month refrigerated.

Lamb

½ cup honey
1 cup Worcestershire sauce

4 12- to 14-ounce lamb racks

In a large bowl, whisk together honey and Worcestershire. Dip lamb in the honey mixture and sear for a couple of minutes on each side on a gas or electric grill. Watch carefully, as the honey glaze burns easily. Remove lamb from grill and place on a rack in a roasting pan in a 425-degree oven for 20 to 30 minutes until done.

To serve, let meat rest for 5 minutes, then slice between each rack with a sharp knife. Arrange on a platter and serve with Horseradish-Mint Sauce on the side. Serves 4.

Glen-Ella Springs Inn's
Apple Bread Pudding with Cinnamon Ice Cream

Cinnamon Ice Cream

½ gallon vanilla ice cream,
  softened
1 tablespoon ground cinnamon

3 tablespoons sugar
2 tablespoons apple schnapps
  or apple juice

Combine all ingredients thoroughly with a mixer and freeze.

Apple Bread Pudding

3 cups apples, peeled and
  chopped fine
³/4 cup light brown sugar
¹/3 cup apple schnapps or apple juice
6 cups stale biscuits
  or coarse bread, crumbled
¹/3 cup raisins

³/4 cup dried apricots, dates,
  or other dried fruits, chopped
3 cups half-and-half
4 eggs, slightly beaten
1½ tablespoons vanilla extract
1 cup sugar
8-ounce jar butterscotch sauce

Preheat oven to 350 degrees. In a small, shallow pan, combine apples with brown sugar and schnapps or apple juice and bake for 20 minutes until sugar melts and apples are tender. Toss apple mixture with crumbled bread and dried fruits and place in a large, well-greased baking pan. Combine remaining ingredients except butterscotch sauce and pour over bread. Bake 30 minutes until custard is set and golden brown.

Serve warm. Cut the custard into 12 squares, place each square in a shallow bowl, and top with a scoop of Cinnamon Ice Cream and butterscotch sauce. Serves 12.

Rudolph's on Green Street

700 Green Street
GAINESVILLE

Some of us grew up in English Tudor houses, and some of us only wish we had. Either group would delight in dining at Rudolph's and relishing the ambiance and the food to which we would like to become accustomed. The outside is all wide, green lawns and flagged patios. The inside abounds with dark wood and Oriental rugs and has an enviable collection of Duncan Phyfe furniture, not to mention four tile fireplaces. A wraparound porch has been cleverly converted into a dining area and bar that, while maintaining the tone of the place, has enough track lighting and other modern amenities to guarantee it doesn't feel too much like Sunday dinner at Great-Aunt Matilda's.

Dinner

5:30 P.M. until 10:00 P.M.
Monday through Thursday

6:00 P.M. until 11:00 P.M.
Friday and Saturday

Lounge opens at 5:00 P.M.

For reservations
call (770) 534-2226

The service is relaxed and easy, as it should be. You can come here in your elegant best, and if you do, remember to pause and admire yourself in the enormous mirror by the wine cellar. On the other hand, if you should be on your way to, say, Lake Lanier and wearing your sailing togs, you would still be welcome and made to feel at home.

At Rudolph's, you can have a glass of wine and dine lightly on Chicken Salad or, if you're feeling extravagant—and thin—indulge in everything from Onion Soup Gratinée to Chocolate Pecan Pie, at which point you will begin to understand why the women who originally lived in English Tudor houses wore corsets. The Filet au Poivre and Roast Duck are house specialties, but whatever you order, have the Rolls or Muffins. They are scrumptious. And come on Saturday night, when there is entertainment.

If after dining at Rudolph's you feel overcome with ennui or, more likely, a desire to work off some calories, take a stroll up and down Green Street. The broad, tree-lined street is flanked by historic homes and sweet-smelling gardens. It is one of the loveliest streets you'll ever wander.

Rudolph's Roast Duck with "Shadows of the Teche" Sauce

"Shadows of the Teche" Sauce

⅓ cup orange juice

¼ cup lemon juice

1 cup powdered sugar

2 tablespoons currant jelly

grated rind of 1 lemon

1 tablespoon horseradish

Combine ingredients and mix until smooth, beating well. Heat over low heat. This sauce may be made the preceding day and kept in the refrigerator. Be sure to bring it to room temperature before heating to serve.

Roast Duck

salt and pepper to taste

4 large ducks

1 medium onion,
    peeled and quartered

1 apple, cored and quartered

1 orange, quartered

2 stalks celery, cut in pieces

¼ cup melted butter

Dry, then salt and pepper the ducks inside and out. Stuff each cavity with an onion quarter, an apple quarter, an orange quarter, and celery. Place in a large roasting pan, leaving space among ducks. Roast at 325 degrees for 15 minutes. Remove excess grease from pan and baste ducks with butter. Continue basting every 15 minutes during cooking. A large duck will be cooked rare in approximately 40 minutes, medium in an hour, and well done in 1½ hours. A small duck will be rare in approximately 30 minutes, medium in 40 minutes, and well done in 50 minutes.

Glaze ducks with "Shadows of the Teche" Sauce in the final minutes of roasting. Serve with the remaining sauce on the side. Serves 8.

Rudolph's Chocolate Pecan Pie

3 eggs

½ cup sugar

½ stick butter, melted

1 teaspoon vanilla extract

½ cup flour

1¼ cups chopped pecans

1 cup chocolate minichips

9-inch piecrust (favorite recipe)

vanilla ice cream (optional)

Lightly whip eggs with an electric mixer set on low speed. Add sugar, butter, and vanilla and mix until thoroughly combined. Add flour gradually and mix until blended. Turn mixer to medium speed and add pecans and chocolate chips. When blended, pour into unbaked pie shell and bake in a 350-degree oven for 30 to 45 minutes. Serve warm, with a scoop of vanilla ice cream if desired. Yields 1 pie.

The Woodbridge Inn

411 Chambers Street
JASPER

he Woodbridge Inn was not serving lunch the first day I went by to visit its owners, the Ruefferts. Nevertheless, car after car drove up to the porch. "We drove fifty miles!" people said. "We drove a hundred miles!" Joe Rueffert gave them directions to other eateries nearby.

"What is it about your place?" I said, having heard even in jaded Atlanta that The Woodbridge Inn is special.

"I buy the best," said Rueffert. "No shortcuts, all fresh food. But it's no use for me to buy the best ingredients if the food is not eaten immediately. Food is at its height the moment it comes off the stove. After that . . . " He shrugged. "So when I have a meal prepared and I say 'Pick up!' my waiters run!"

Lunch

11:00 A.M. until 2:00 P.M.
Wednesday

11:00 A.M. until 4:00 P.M.
Sunday

Dinner

5:30 P.M. until 9:00 P.M.
Monday through Thursday

5:00 P.M. until 10:00 P.M.
Friday and Saturday

4:00 P.M. until 8:00 P.M.
Sunday

For reservations
(recommended)
call (706) 692-6293

He made it sound so easy, I rhapsodized for days that I had found the secret to a perfect meal: fleet-footed service. Then I remembered that Joe Rueffert had modestly ignored his European training. During several visits, I discovered that his best is considerably better than mine. I could roller-skate to the dinner table and my Rainbow Trout wouldn't be as succulent as his. Nor would my Filet Mignon Forestière, Crabmeat Gratinée, Peach Melba, or Lemon Cream Pie ever quite match his. Nevertheless, the two recipes which follow have been happily received by my friends and family and will no doubt be similarly received by yours. Be advised that these are not standard recipes for familiar dishes. This may be because Joe himself doesn't use the recipes anymore. "Oh, no. I just cook it until it's right."

The restaurant used to be Ed Lenning's inn. He started it with the proceeds from his gold strike in California and ran it for years, taking time out to fight as a Confederate soldier in the Civil War. When the railroad came through Jasper, it passed in front of the inn, which then became a haven for Floridians escaping to the mountains for the summer. Today, the lodge's twelve beautiful rooms overlooking northern Georgia's peaks are a treat not to be missed.

The restaurant is not decorated as a period piece. The tone is European. If you have ever spent time in the southern Alps or northern Italy and miss the ambiance, you'll love this place. It's clean and green, with homespun tablecloths topped with white linen and flowers. If you arrive before dusk, you can sip your wine and nibble your salad while watching the sun set over the mountains, and you'll understand why the inn has lured such a succession of weary travelers to its bed and board.

The Woodbridge Inn's Oysters Rockefeller

Hollandaise Sauce

1 stick butter	1 tablespoon lemon juice
1 egg yolk	dash of cayenne pepper
1 tablespoon boiling water	dash of salt

Melt the butter. Put egg yolk into a blender and, while blending slowly, add boiling water and lemon juice. Pour in butter in a thin, continuous stream. Add cayenne pepper and salt. Yields ¾ cup.

Oysters

10 ounces fresh spinach	½ teaspoon garlic salt
2 stalks celery	½ teaspoon white pepper
1 small onion	dash of Pernod
½ jalapeño pepper	24 oysters
1 clove garlic	½ cup Parmesan and
2 tablespoons butter	Romano cheeses, grated fine
1 tablespoon soy sauce	

Chop spinach and cook it in water until tender, then remove from heat and let sit for a few minutes. Mince celery, onion, jalapeño, and garlic; sauté them in butter until soft. Drain spinach and add it to the celery mixture. Stir in soy sauce, garlic salt, white pepper, and Pernod.

Shuck oysters and place them, on the half-shell, in a casserole or baking pan. Put them in a 350-degree oven until shells are hot. Then put a spoonful of spinach mixture on each oyster, top with Hollandaise, and sprinkle with Parmesan and Romano. Place oysters under the broiler until brown. Serves 6 as an appetizer.

The Woodbridge Inn's Seafood à la Newburg

1 stick butter
6 tablespoons flour
1½ cups chicken broth
¼ cup dry sherry
4 tablespoons Hungarian paprika
2 stalks celery, diced
1 onion, diced
1 clove garlic, diced
1 jalapeño pepper, diced (no seeds)

½ pound shrimp,
    peeled and deveined
½ pound scallops
¼ pound crabmeat, picked
2 ounces cognac
1 cup grated mozzarella,
    mild cheddar, and Swiss cheeses,
    mixed

Make a roux by melting 5 tablespoons of the butter, adding the flour, and stirring over low heat for a few minutes until honey colored. Add chicken stock, stirring continuously until thickened. Add sherry and paprika and let simmer. Put half the remaining butter in a frying pan and sauté celery, onion, garlic, and jalapeño until glazed. Add the mixture to the thickened stock. Sauté the seafood in the rest of the butter until shrimp turn pink; add seafood and cognac to the stock. Pour the mixture into a casserole or individual ramekins and top with cheeses. Broil until cheeses bubble and brown. Serves 2 to 4.

Lickskillet Farm

Old Roswell Road
ALPHARETTA

*O*ne of the charms of the Atlanta suburbs is the little enclaves flourishing among them. One minute, you're surrounded by discount stores and miles of pavement, but turn a corner, go around a bend, and voilà! You're greeted by rolling hills sprinkled with trees, watered by a meandering brook, and here and there dotted with cows. In such a niche is Lickskillet Farm, complete with a Civil War entrenchment in the backyard, down by Foekiller Creek.

Today, Lickskillet Farm's ambiance is more country French than country Georgia. The brick-floored foyer, the scattered watercolors, an apple tree stenciled on the sun porch wall—these are soothing, carefree reminders that eating out is the life you were born to.

Lunch
11:30 A.M. until 2:00 P.M.
Tuesday through Friday

Dinner
6:00 P.M. until 10:00 P.M.
Monday through Friday

5:30 P.M. until 10:00 P.M.
Saturday

5:30 P.M. until 9:00 P.M.
Sunday

Brunch
10:30 A.M. until 2:00 P.M.
Sunday

For reservations
(recommended)
call (770) 475-6484

Say you go for Sunday brunch. It begins, promisingly enough, with champagne—or coffee or tea, if you prefer. Then you can sidle nonchalantly up to the buffet, where a variety of delights awaits you. My favorite ploy is to pretend I'm having breakfast—Scrambled Eggs with Sour Cream and Chives, Roasted Garlic Cheese Grits, mounds of fresh fruit, Belgian Waffles with Raspberry Jam. Then I rest a bit, watching the birds out the window. Then I start over with lunch. My son goes straight for the Dijon Mustard Creamed Potatoes and the Chicken Drummettes, returning as often as necessary to those dishes alone, with an occasional foray to the Leg of Lamb being carved in the corner.

After enjoying dessert and coffee while listening to the music from the grand piano by the fireplace, you may want to contemplate your next visit. An anniversary, perhaps? Lickskillet Farm is a good place to bring the friends you wish you had time to entertain at home.

That's the charm of the place. You feel that dining at home ought to be like this. And it would be, too, if only you had the time. And the talent. And the recipes. And a gentleman to play your piano.

Lickskillet Farm's Southern Cornbread

3 eggs
½ cup sour cream
¼ cup oil
14-ounce can cream-style corn

3 tablespoons sugar
3 tablespoons bacon,
   chopped and cooked
1¼ cups self-rising cornmeal

Combine first 6 ingredients in a mixing bowl. Add cornmeal and mix well; do not allow to lump. Oil two 6-inch cast-iron skillets and fill ¾ full with cornbread mixture. Bake in a 350-degree oven for 30 to 40 minutes until a toothpick inserted in the center comes out clean. Serve hot with butter and honey. Serves 4 to 6.

Lickskillet Farm's Snapper Alicia

Hollandaise Sauce

2 egg yolks
½ cup clarified butter
½ lemon

3 drops Tabasco sauce
salt and cayenne pepper to taste

In the top of a double boiler over low heat, whisk egg yolks until smooth and creamy. Add butter slowly, allowing ingredients to emulsify. Squeeze lemon into the sauce, add Tabasco, and sprinkle with salt and cayenne pepper.

Snapper

4 6-ounce Gulf red snapper fillets
salt and pepper to taste
garlic powder to taste
4 tablespoons butter
1 cup all-purpose flour
¼ cup white wine

3 tablespoons lemon juice
¼ cup chicken stock
8 ounces jumbo lump crabmeat
1 tablespoon chopped shallots
1 pound fresh spinach

Preheat oven to 350 degrees. Rinse fillets, pat dry with a paper towel, and sprinkle with salt and pepper and garlic powder. Heat 3 tablespoons of the butter in a large, ovenproof sauté skillet on medium heat. Dredge snapper in flour and sauté on both sides for 3 minutes. Deglaze pan by adding wine and stirring gently. Add lemon juice and chicken stock and place skillet in oven for 10 minutes until snapper is cooked thoroughly. Drain crabmeat and pick out shell bits. Add crabmeat to snapper and set aside. In another sauté pan, heat remaining tablespoon of butter on medium-high, add shallots and spinach, and season with salt and pepper and garlic powder. Cook until wilted; place equal portions on 4 plates. Heat snapper and crabmeat.

To serve, place fillets over spinach, pour remaining sauce and crabmeat over snapper, and finish with a dollop of Hollandaise. Serves 4.

Lickskillet Farm's Roasted Garlic Cheese Grits

9 cups water
¾ teaspoon salt
2¼ cups instant grits

4 ounces cheddar cheese, grated
4 tablespoons garlic,
*   roasted and chopped*

Bring water to a boil in a medium saucepan, add salt, and stir in grits. Return to a boil. Cover and reduce heat to simmer. Cook 5 minutes, stirring occasionally. Add cheese and garlic and stir until cheese is melted. Serves 8.

The Public House
on Roswell Square

605 South Atlantic Street
ROSWELL

reek Indians lived in the Chattahoochee River basin 160 years ago. They fished and hunted and chased off a few trespassing settlers, for which crime they were invited to resettle several states westward. Then, in 1837, Roswell King and friends came to the Chattahoochee basin and built a series of cotton mills and a little town named, appropriately enough, Roswell. It was a charming place, boasting among other things a company store, in which employees of the mills could purchase goods on credit. Everything was sold in such stores—food, hardware, wood, cloth, even coffins. In the Roswell Company Store, you could even get your teeth pulled.

Lunch
11:30 A.M. until 2:30 P.M.
Monday through Friday

11:30 A.M. until 3:00 P.M.
Saturday and Sunday

Dinner
5:30 P.M. until 10:00 P.M.
Monday through Thursday

5:30 P.M. until 11:00 P.M.
Friday and Saturday

5:30 P.M. until 9:00 P.M.
Sunday

Reservations are not taken.

For information
call (770) 992-4646

Today, the same building houses something a good deal more pleasant than a dentist's office—The Public House on Roswell Square. For twenty-plus years now, this restaurant has been a source of joy and succor to its many friends.

Some people visit The Public House only at night, because they like to go upstairs and sit at the bar, soaking up the pub life which predominates. Others maintain that lunchtime is when the place is its most delightful. I vote for rainy Saturdays myself. The restaurant's cream-and-tan-striped awnings are easy to spot in a downpour, and there is a cozy entrance in which to shake off your umbrella. The walls of glossy white plaster and rough brick, the crisp linen tablecloths, the willowware, and the fresh flowers make you feel less wet and frazzled.

The food here lends a feeling of welcome. During our last visit, my husband ordered the Lump Crab Cakes—three sautéed crab cakes served with a smoked corn and calypso bean ragout. I chose the Pot Pie—broccoli, beans, carrots, and chicken with a corn spoonbread crust. It's a perfect rainy-day comfort food. And the Grilled Veal

Chops with Green Tomato Jus and Crispy Red Onions are now for us a Saturday-evening-at-home staple.

After lunch, which was perfect, I sneaked up the stairs to the then-deserted pub room, hoping to see the resident ghosts. They are Katherine and her lover, Michael, a seventeen-year-old Union soldier who reportedly died here during the Civil War, when the building served as a field hospital before returning to its life as a store. All offers to have the pair exorcised have been refused by the managers, who are comfortable with Katherine and Michael if Katherine and Michael are comfortable with them. The ghosts could certainly do a lot worse.

The Public House's Grilled Veal Chops with Green Tomato Jus and Crispy Red Onions

Green Tomato Jus

2 stalks Vidalia green onions
  (white part), chopped fine
1 tablespoon olive oil
3 cloves garlic, mashed
¼ cup white wine
2 green tomatoes, diced fine

2 cups chicken or veal stock
½ teaspoon fresh thyme, chopped
½ teaspoon marjoram
½ teaspoon basil
½ teaspoon cilantro
salt and pepper to taste

Sauté onions in olive oil until golden brown. Add garlic. Deglaze with wine. Add tomatoes and cook slowly until semisoft. Add stock and seasonings and simmer until reduced by half. Sauce should be a smooth consistency, with chunks of tomato.

Crispy Red Onions

⅛ teaspoon cumin
⅛ teaspoon salt
⅛ teaspoon pepper

¼ cup flour
¼ red onion, sliced thin

Mix cumin, salt, and pepper into flour. Dust onions with flour mixture and deep-fry at 375 degrees until golden brown.

Veal chops

salt and pepper to taste   *2 veal chops*

Salt and pepper veal chops and grill them for 3 to 4 minutes on each side until done.

To serve, place veal chops on individual plates and top with Green Tomato Jus and Crispy Red Onions. Serve with pearl barley pilaf and sautéed collard greens if desired. Serves 2.

1848 House

780 South Cobb Drive
MARIETTA

People come to Atlanta all the time wanting to see Scarlett's house from *Gone With the Wind*. It isn't here, because for one thing Scarlett wasn't a real person. If she had been a real person, you probably still couldn't see her house, because Sherman would have burned it in 1865 along with everything else. That's the reason Atlanta is such a postbellum, "skyscraperish" sort of place. You can go for miles without seeing a single white-columned

mansion. But if you're determined, you can find one in the suburbs, and it's the real thing, too. It's called the 1848 House. If Scarlett had been an actual person, she would have gone to parties here, flounced up and down the stairs, and kissed Rhett (or Ashley) in one of the parlors or under the magnolias in the yard.

The 1848 House was known as Bushy Park when it was part of a three-thousand-acre plantation owned by Charlestonian John Glover, who became mayor of Marietta. The seventeen-room Greek Revival home no doubt saw many glittering parties in its day. By the time Sherman came calling, Sarah and William King lived here. Mr. King hid his children in the cellar and watched the Federal cavalrymen coming up the road, taking many casualties as they advanced. After the battle, Federal forces chose Bushy Park as a hospital for the wounded, thus sparing it for future generations.

The house has atmosphere galore. Meticulously maintained, it has enough period antiques—some original to the house—to give it an authentic flavor. If you're into history, it's here. The original land grant hangs in the upstairs hallway. My favorite historian's touch is the mural in the Garrison Dining Room, a modern depiction of the view from the top of Big Kennesaw Mountain as it appeared in 1848.

When you're through gawking, you can eat, and thus receive two treats for the price of one. You will dine on contemporary Southern food, beginning perhaps with Steamed Mussels or She-Crab Soup, proceeding to Blue Cheese and Pear Salad, Grilled Salmon with Red

Pepper, or perhaps Loin of Lamb or Roasted Venison. And over dessert—perhaps Green Apple Gratin with Warm Nutmeg Cream—you can gaze out at the rose garden or the stars twinkling through the magnolias and thank God that, unlike Scarlett, you don't have to worry about an eighteen-inch waist.

1848 House's Green Apple Gratin with Warm Nutmeg Cream

Nutmeg Cream

2 cups heavy cream
¼ cup butter
½ teaspoon freshly ground nutmeg

½ cup sugar
¼ teaspoon salt

Combine all ingredients in a saucepan. Simmer over low heat, whisking occasionally, until reduced to 2½ cups. Transfer to a blender or food processor and blend until texture is smooth.

Streusel

¾ cup plus 2 tablespoons flour
¾ cup sugar
¾ teaspoons cinnamon

⅛ teaspoon salt
3 tablespoons butter

Put all dry ingredients into a mixing bowl and stir until combined. Add butter and blend with fingers or paddle attachment of mixer until the consistency of fine sand.

Spice Mix and Apples

¹/₄ cup sugar
¹/₂ teaspoon cinnamon
¹/₂ teaspoon nutmeg
¹/₈ teaspoon ground cloves

¹/₈ teaspoon salt
6 tart green apples
1 pint vanilla ice cream

Combine sugar, spices, and salt in a large bowl. Cut the apples into quarters, peel, remove cores, and slice apples lengthwise. Toss the apple slices with the spice mix. Arrange a single layer of apple slices in 6 buttered au gratin dishes. Pour 1 tablespoon Nutmeg Cream over each dish and top with $^{1}/_{6}$ of the streusel mix. Bake at 350 degrees until apples are soft and streusel is golden.

Serve warm with a scoop of vanilla ice cream and 2 ounces of warm Nutmeg Cream. Serves 6.

1848 House's Maytag Blue Cheese and Pear Salad

1 ounce aged sherry wine vinegar
4 ounces extra-virgin olive oil
coarse salt and fresh pepper
  to taste

6 ounces mixed greens, fresh
6 ounces Maytag blue cheese
3 ripe pears

Bring blue cheese to room temperature. Make a vinaigrette by combining vinegar, olive oil, and salt and pepper in a covered jar; shake well. Taste vinaigrette; if too acid, add a scant teaspoon of honey. Set aside. Rinse greens in cold water, drain, and shake off remaining water. Halve the pears, remove cores, and slice pears into strips. Toss them in the vinaigrette and set aside. Toss greens in vinaigrette and mound them in the center of 6 salad plates. Arrange the pears around greens; adjust seasonings. Garnish salads with crumbles of blue cheese. Serves 6.

Maximillian's

1857 Airport Industrial Park Avenue
MARIETTA

The next time you find yourself negotiating I-75 during rush hour in Atlanta, spare a millisecond to glance northward. In the late 1920s, a Marietta lawyer built himself a hunting lodge a few miles from you. His name was James Carmichael, and he owned much of the land thereabouts and wanted a quiet retreat from which to sally forth into the woods with his guns on crisp autumn mornings. (The woods are part of what is now Dobbins Air Force Base.) Carmichael liked his little place so well that he finally moved into it full time, adding along the way a swimming pool and electricity—the first of either to grace a private residence in Cobb County.

The hunting lodge is now a restaurant called Maximillian's. It looks like a mountain house, all shingles and stone, tucked into the side of a hill. Small paneled rooms follow each other in comfortable succession; the atmosphere is intimate and secluded. There's a large stone fireplace which on chilly days has a fire in it. Downstairs are a stone-floored bar and a lounge overlooking the pool, now a home for ducks. The pool isn't like the ones built these days. It's a cement pond, sort of, built as a holding pool for a stream in the days before chlorination. I have always wanted to swim in an old-fashioned pool like this, and someday I might just drink too many "Maximillian's Coffees" and give those complacent ducks a run for their money.

Meanwhile, I can easily content myself with Fresh Mahi-Mahi Macadamia, Beef Tenderloin au Poivre, or Veal à la Oscar. Or if I'm in a more adventurous mood, I can tackle the Colorado Elk Chop or Emu Marsala. Maximillian's serves the largest variety of exotic game in the Southeast. Just the sort of adventure James Carmichael would have enjoyed.

Maximillian's Stuffed Grouper

Crabmeat Stuffing

1 egg
1 tablespoon half-and-half
2 tablespoons mayonnaise
½ teaspoon Old Bay seasoning
  (or crab boil)
½ tablespoon Worcestershire sauce
½ teaspoon white pepper

½ teaspoon salt
1½ tablespoons pimientos
2 tablespoons parsley flakes
2 tablespoons finely chopped onion
2 tablespoons finely chopped
  green pepper
1 pound blue crabmeat

Mix all ingredients well, adding the crabmeat last. This mixture can be used to stuff fish, avocados, or mushrooms.

salt and pepper to taste
6 8-ounce grouper fillets

1 cup hollandaise sauce (see index)

Salt and pepper the fillets and spoon ⅙ of the stuffing onto the center of each one. Fold the ends of each fillet over and place fillets in a baking dish. Bake at 325 degrees for 15 or 20 minutes until creamy white.

Top each fillet with hollandaise before serving. Serves 6.

Maximillian's Coffee

1½ ounces Irish whiskey
1 ounce Tia Maria
1 ounce Grand Marnier

6 ounces coffee
2 ounces fresh whipped cream

Blend first 4 ingredients in a serving mug. Top with whipped cream. Serves 1.

Maximillian's Carrots Au Grand Marnier

1½ pounds carrots
2 cups orange juice

1 cup brown sugar
1 ounce Grand Marnier

Peel and slice carrots and parboil them until tender. Stir together orange juice, brown sugar, and Grand Marnier, then add drained carrots.

Marinate in the refrigerator 24 hours. Reheat carrots in their marinade to serve. Serves 4 to 6.

Maximillian's Cream of Mushroom Soup

1 pound fresh mushrooms, sliced
4 cups water
4 cups heavy cream
1½ cups or less sherry
½ teaspoon white pepper

4 tablespoons chicken base
or bouillon
1½ sticks butter
6 tablespoons flour

Cook the mushrooms in the water until tender. Add cream, sherry, pepper, and chicken base and bring to a boil. Meanwhile, make a roux in a sauté pan by melting the butter and stirring in flour. Heat, stirring, until the flour has cooked and turned light brown. Add the roux to the boiling soup a little at a time, adding only what is necessary to thicken soup to your taste. Serves 4.

The Mansion

179 Ponce de Leon Avenue
ATLANTA

By the 1880s, Atlanta had partially recovered from the unpleasantness with Sherman's army and was undergoing a building boom to reflect its new status as the state capital. Philadelphia railroad man Richard Peters was building, too. He liked the area where Ponce de Leon Avenue is today. It was all a forest then, and he thought the wood would make good fuel for his flour mill. So he bought four hundred acres of it for five dollars an acre, and he built himself a mansion in the middle of it—a Victorian shingle-style house which reflected, architecturally, his Philadelphia heritage. It was enormous, rambling, loaded with charming nooks and crannies.

Lunch
11:30 A.M. until 2:30 P.M.
Monday through Friday

Dinner
6:00 P.M. until 11:00 P.M.
Every day

Brunch
11:30 A.M. until 2:30 P.M.
Saturday and Sunday

For reservations
(recommended)
call (404) 876-0727

The Victorians knew a lot about using contrasts of texture and color to add drama to a house, and The Mansion provides a short course in the technique. Where dark wood can lead up to a sparkling leaded-glass window, it does. Where a hall can unexpectedly provide an opportunity for a tête-à-tête, it will. There are eleven dining rooms in all, and each is completely different from the next. The whole atmosphere is unexpectedly rich and festive. The lobby and the spacious gazebo—a bar featuring nightly entertainment—are recent additions, serene and airy. The courtyard—a dining area which overlooks a lovely fountain—emits just the right amount of careless elegance. On spring Saturdays, you are likely to glimpse a wedding out there.

The Mansion's European-trained chef innovatively combines Old World and Southern cuisine. You can savor his Grilled Shrimp Cocktail with Mustard Sauce, Boneless Broiled Duck with Beans, and extraordinary Chocolate Pâté, which won the 1987 "Best Dessert in Atlanta" award. The Oriental Chicken Salad looks truly sophisticated, but it brings out the worst in people. I had to slap my cousin's hand three times to keep her fingers out of my plate.

If, while paying your bill in the atrium, you hear an unearthly scream in the wall behind the cash register, don't assume it's a fellow diner being tortured for his charge-card number. It's the parrot getting acquainted with one of the guests. You'll want to get acquainted with The Mansion—and perhaps with its resident parrot—the next time you're in Atlanta.

The Mansion's Chocolate Paté

*1 pound bittersweet chocolate
    (Eidelweiss or Lindt,
    not baking chocolate)
1½ cups brandy
3 to 4 sticks butter
¼ pound white chocolate
    (Eidelweiss or Lindt)*

*2 tablespoons water
½ pound pecans
15 egg yolks
¼ cup mint jelly
fresh fruit
whipped cream (optional)*

In a double boiler over simmering water, melt the bittersweet chocolate with 1 cup brandy and 3 sticks butter; if it seems too thick, add a little more butter. Remove from heat and let cool to room temperature. Also in a double boiler over simmering heat, melt the white chocolate with ½ cup brandy and 2 tablespoons water; if white chocolate needs to be thinned (it should be relatively thick), add a little more water. Remove from heat and let cool to room temperature.

Grind the pecans very fine. In a separate bowl, stir the egg yolks. Whip pecans and yolks into the dark chocolate. Oil a loaf pan well and pour half the dark chocolate into it. Make a channel with a spoon down the middle of the chocolate without touching either end of the pan. Pour the white chocolate into this channel. Ladle a stream of mint jelly on top of the white chocolate and cover it with the rest of the dark chocolate. Allow the chocolate to chill in the refrigerator for 2 to 4 hours, then fold it out of the mold.

To serve, slice the chocolate as if you're slicing a loaf of bread and lay it in dessert plates with fresh fruit. If desired, top with whipped cream. Serves 10 to 12.

Miso Dressing

½ cup teriyaki sauce
¾ cup white wine
1 tablespoon olive oil
1 bay leaf

dash of salt and pepper
dash of garlic
1 teaspoon fresh ginger or
½ teaspoon dried ginger

Mix all ingredients together and refrigerate overnight. Remove bay leaf before serving.

Salad

4 whole chicken breasts
3 or 4 raw carrots
1 green pepper
1 red bell pepper

2 cups snow peas
1 cup water chestnuts
lettuce leaves
tofu for garnish

Grill chicken breasts and set them aside to cool. Peel and julienne carrots and slice peppers and snow peas. Blanch carrots, peppers, and snow peas for 30 seconds in boiling water and set aside. Slice water chestnuts and set them aside. Pull the chicken apart into bite-size pieces and combine it with the vegetables. Toss with Miso Dressing and chill.

Serve on lettuce leaves garnished with tofu. Serves 4 to 6.

Anthony's Plantation Restaurant

3109 Piedmont Road
ATLANTA

𝒜 tlantans, when queried by out-of-towners about a good place to eat, tend to shrug and mutter defensively that it all depends. That's because there are several hundred restaurants in Atlanta, and it really does depend. If you press them, however—if you say, "I want an Old South experience, good food, and lush sur-

roundings, and I don't mind paying for them"—they will probably mention Anthony's.

When you see the lovely old 1797 plantation house, tucked out of sight behind a doctor's office, you won't believe it's been here two hundred years. And it hasn't. For most of its life, it stood in Washington, Georgia, until it was dismantled and moved, brick by painstaking brick, to its present site. It's a plain-style plantation house. The two central halls, downstairs and upstairs, were originally open walk-throughs providing cross-ventilation and a wonderful place to get out of the sun on hot afternoons. Nowadays, all is enclosed and air-conditioned, but the feel of early-nineteenth-century Southern life is unmistakable. The old kitchen, complete with fireplace, is all brick. The front rooms are loaded with Chippendale country English pieces and oil paintings. Behind the bar is the old stone-floored wine cellar, where a group may dine in privacy. My personal favorite is the upstairs porch, where guests can look out over the grounds and pretend to be master of all they survey.

The food here is special. Anthony's has been named one of the top ten continental restaurants in the United States by the American Academy of Restaurant Sciences every year since 1993, so bring your appetite. How about Southern Fried Quail, Country-Style Smoked Pork and Chicken Liver Pâté, or Soused Salmon to start? These are true Southern specialties adapted from two-hundred-year-old recipes. Among the entrées, the Chateaubriand is excellent, or you might prefer fowl or fish any one of five or six ways. If you're a vegetarian, no problem—there's always something truly original and delicious on the menu for you, like Twice-Baked Crookneck Squash with Creole-Style Vegetable Medley. For dessert, dare I mention the Bananas Foster, Bourbon Pecan Pie, and Strawberries Romanoff?

And if you have cab fare home, try a Frankly My Dear—a heady blend of brandy, rum, Southern Comfort, orange juice, and champagne. If Scarlett had had the good sense to offer Rhett one of these on his way out the door, he'd probably still be there, fumbling for his coat.

Anthony's Plantation Restaurant's Country-Style Smoked Pork and Chicken Liver Pâté

3 pounds chicken livers
½ cup vegetable oil
1½ pounds smoked pork, cubed
1 cup brandy
3 shallots, peeled and chopped
1 tablespoon salt

1 tablespoon freshly ground pepper
1½ teaspoons chopped garlic
½ teaspoon freshly grated nutmeg
1 cup sour cream
4 medium eggs, beaten

Clean connective tissues from livers. Heat oil in a skillet and brown livers over high heat until colored; do not overcook. Drain fat. Cover and refrigerate 1/3 of livers. In a medium bowl, combine the remaining 2/3 of the livers with smoked pork, brandy, and shallots. Cover and marinate in the refrigerator at least 6 hours or overnight.

Using a food processor or meat grinder, process the meat mixture, including the marinade, through a fine blade. Add salt, pepper, garlic, and nutmeg. Stir in sour cream. Beat in eggs 1 at a time until well blended. Line bottom and sides of a 9-by-5-inch loaf pan with wax paper or parchment. Butter sides of pan. Place 1/3 of the meat mixture in bottom of pan and top with half of the reserved livers. Top with another layer of meat mixture and livers and end with the meat mix. Place the loaf pan in a larger pan and add hot water to half the height of the pan. Bake at 325 degrees for 2 hours until juices run clear. Remove from oven and place a piece of foil-wrapped cardboard over the pâté. Weigh it down with a 2-pound weight or a few vegetable cans. Refrigerate overnight.

To serve, invert the pâté onto a platter and slice. Serves 14 to 16.

Anthony's Plantation Restaurant's Soused Salmon

rock salt

3-pound fresh salmon fillet, skin on

1 fennel bulb, chopped fine

1 leek, chopped fine

12 white peppercorns, crushed

2 bay leaves, crushed

5 branches fresh thyme,
   chopped coarse

juice of 10 fresh limes

½ cup red wine vinegar

Lay rock salt in a pan large enough to hold salmon; use enough salt to cover bottom of pan completely. Lay salmon skin side down on the salt. Mix remaining ingredients together and let stand 15 minutes. Drain the liquid and set it aside. Carefully place leek mixture on salmon. Pour ¼ of reserved liquid over leek mixture, cover, and place in the refrigerator. Let stand 4 hours, then add more liquid, repeating the procedure until all the liquid has been used. Cover pan tightly and do not disturb for 24 to 36 hours. Remove salmon, discard everything else, slice paper-thin, and serve. Serves 6 or more.

Atkins Park Restaurant

794 North Highland Avenue
ATLANTA

In 1925, the Atlanta suburb of Virginia Highlands was an exceedingly nice place to live—a bit far out, to be sure, but the streetcar ran right downtown, and the houses were the latest style. At Atkins Park, there was even a small commercial district with shops and a little delicatessen. On a nice day, you could stroll down to the market or, if you preferred, order something delivered. The atmosphere was refined—peaceful suburbia with style.

Virginia Highlands is still an exceedingly nice place to live—a tad close in, maybe, but the houses are really adorable, and it's just minutes from everywhere. The kids can practically walk to school. Plus, it has all the perks—

bookstores, shops, and a variety of restaurants you can wander through for a bite on your way home from work or play.

Take Atkins Park Restaurant, for instance. The building used to be a deli in the 1920s, then became a tavern—and has been one ever since. It is the oldest continuously licensed tavern in Atlanta, although it currently houses a first-class restaurant, too. You enter the restaurant through the bar, still adorned with tin ceiling and tile floor. Booths line one wall, and you can eat there if you like, or even outside in the little alleyway beside the building, a popular place to have a beer on springtime evenings. For dinner, though, you might prefer the dining room, with its brick walls and old pine booths and tables.

The food at Atkins Park is bar food in the best sense of the term—food to savor, soups and noshes. The munchies include something called Mucho Nachos—a mountain of tortilla chips smothered with beans, cheese, salsa, guacamole, jalapeños, and so on. And then there are the burgers. Atkins Park makes one of the best hamburgers in Atlanta. It's called the Buff Burger, and it's a simple meat-lettuce-tomato-onion affair with Fries. Order extra Fries to keep your friends from eating all of yours.

For dinner, you might start with Crab Cakes or Cioppino, a prizewinning seafood soup in a spicy tomato broth, then proceed to Chicken Mezcal, Australian Rack of Lamb, Open-Faced Lasagna, or Atkins Park Fillet, topped with Blue Cheese Butter. Or you can just nibble Southwestern Quesadillas all night.

While sipping your coffee, note the two stained-glass phoenixes, the restaurant logo, and the pictures of old Atlanta which adorn the walls. It's a great way to absorb a history lesson.

Atkins Park Restaurant's Southwestern Quesadillas

½ cup black olives
¼ cup jalapeños
4-ounce can green chilis
1 tablespoon margarine
12 ounces diced chicken breast
   or shrimp
1½ cups corn salsa
salt and pepper to taste

12 6-inch flour tortillas
16 ounces shredded cheddar
   and Monterey Jack cheeses,
   mixed
4 tablespoons salsa
4 tablespoons sour cream
4 tablespoons guacamole

Dice olives, jalapeños, and chilis. Heat in a saucepan. In a sauté pan, melt margarine and sauté chicken or shrimp over medium heat until done. Add corn salsa and salt and pepper and stir until hot. Arrange tortillas 3 at a time on a baking sheet and place under a broiler until lightly browned. Turn them over, sprinkle cheese on top of 2 of them, and continue heating until cheese is melted. Repeat with remaining tortillas. To assemble quesadillas, place one of the cheese tortillas on each of 4 plates. Top with ¼ of the black olive mixture. Top with a second cheese tortilla. Add ¼ of the chicken or shrimp mixture next and top with 1 of the plain tortillas. Garnish with salsa, sour cream, and guacamole. Serves 4.

Note: If you cannot find corn salsa, substitute 1 cup salsa mixed with ½ cup canned whole-kernel corn, drained.

Atkins Park Fillet

Sweet and Sour Onion Marmalade

2 onions, sliced thin   *¼ cup balsamic vinegar*
2 tablespoons brown sugar   *1 tablespoon brown grain mustard*

Sauté onions with brown sugar, vinegar, and mustard until golden brown.

Blue Cheese Butter

¼ pound butter   *1½ ounces crumbled blue cheese*

Soften butter and knead in blue cheese. Roll butter up in a sheet of wax paper and place in the freezer until hard. Cut as needed.

4 steak fillets   *salt and pepper*

Broil, grill, or pan-fry fillets. Add salt and pepper to taste.

To serve, place Sweet and Sour Onion Marmalade on each of 4 plates, add the steaks, and top with a slice of Blue Cheese Butter. Serves 4.

The Abbey

163 Ponce de Leon Avenue
ATLANTA

The Abbey caters to those of us who saw *Becket* three times and cherish a fondness for a medieval atmosphere. Here, you dine in a converted church sanctuary under a fifty-foot vaulted ceiling. Easing into your leather-covered bishop's chair, you take in the gleaming table setting, the fresh flowers. Shadows dance on the walls in the flickering light, and you wish you had worn your velvet. Then a "monkish" waiter brings you a menu and you get down to business, selecting a meal from an incredible array of culinary jewels. The menu is full of delicious-sounding food that could be featured in gourmet magazines—and, in fact, sometimes is. There is Galantine of Duckling with Lingonberries, Spinach and Fois Gras Salad with Hot Bacon Dressing, and Baked Oysters with Scallops and Bay Shrimp. And those are just the appetizers. The entrées include most anything you'd want from a continental menu: fish, fowl, beef, veal, lamb, and venison. And be sure to save room for a Praline Tulip and some Coffee laced with Benedictine. You may waddle home feeling like Charles Laughton playing Henry VIII, but never mind. Unlike Henry, you won't have to get up the next morning and ride to the hounds.

The Abbey has been a renowned Atlanta restaurant since its opening in 1968, earning international food and wine awards all along the way. Formerly a Methodist Episcopal church, the 1915 structure reflects the passion for Renaissance Gothic architecture which dominated the end of the Victorian period. During the day, the massive arched windows let in an abundance of refracted light. And don't get so caught up in your Lobster Thermidor that you fail to notice the stained glass, which is gorgeous, especially the ceiling in the Abbot's Cup Lounge.

Early church fathers appreciated how worshipers' senses became

Cocktail Lounge
Opens at 5:00 P.M.
Daily

Restaurant
Opens at 6:00 P.M.
Daily
Last seating is at 10:45 P.M.

Banquet facilities are available for business luncheons, receptions, and other special events.

For reservations
(recommended)
call (404) 876-8532

more alert in the rich and lofty air of a cathedral. The Abbey works on the same principle. Whatever your experience here, it's certain to be unlike any church supper you've ever had.

The Abbey's French Brie Soup

¼ cup butter
2 cups diced onions
¼ teaspoon diced garlic
1 cup sliced mushrooms
1 cup dry white wine
¼ cup flour
3½ cups chicken stock or broth

1 bay leaf
pinch of freshly chopped thyme
1¼ pints heavy whipping cream
10 ounces Brie, sliced
salt and pepper to taste
2 ounces sherry
12 toasted croutons

Melt butter in a saucepan and sauté onions, garlic, and mushrooms. Add wine and reduce until almost dry. Add flour and work mixture into a paste over low heat. Add chicken stock and bay leaf, bring to a boil, and simmer until a soup consistency is achieved. Add thyme and whipping cream. Strain the soup and replace on heat. Using a whisk, slowly blend in 6 ounces of Brie, whipping until smooth. Add salt and pepper and sherry. Pour soup into bowls, top with croutons, and lay remaining slices of Brie on croutons. Brown lightly under a broiler and serve. Serves 8.

The Abbey's Praline Tulips

Pralines

1 cups light brown sugar
1 cup light Karo syrup
2 sticks unsalted butter
2 cups chopped pecans
   and/or almonds

2 cups flour
parchment paper

Bring sugar, syrup, and butter to a boil over medium heat. Remove from heat. Add nuts and flour to the syrup and mix well. Preheat oven to 325 degrees and prepare sheet pans by covering with parchment and spraying the paper with Pam. Spoon mixture onto the paper, making rounds approximately 6 inches in diameter. Bake for 10 to 15 minutes until pralines can be lifted from the parchment without breaking. When bubbles subside, carefully place pralines on inverted soup cups. They will droop and form a cup. Let them stand until hard. Store pralines in plastic containers between layers of parchment. Yields approximately 15 pralines.

2 pints sliced strawberries   *15 whole pecans for garnish*
½ gallon vanilla ice cream

Just prior to serving, fill pralines with strawberries, top with ice cream, and garnish with one slice of strawberry and one pecan. Serves 15.

The Abbey's Apricot Soup

2 pounds dried apricots   *4 tablespoons lemon juice*
¾ cup Sauterne or Barsac   *1 cup sugar*
6 cups whipping cream   *pinch of salt*
1 cup sour cream   *orange peel and mint leaves*
1 teaspoon cinnamon   *for garnish*
¼ teaspoon nutmeg

Soak apricots overnight in wine and whipping cream; drain and reserve the liquid. Purée apricots and add to the wine mixture. Add sour cream, reserving ¼ cup for garnish; add remaining ingredients except for garnishes. Pass all of this mixture through a cheesecloth to the serving container, discarding the pulp after it has been squeezed dry. Chill and top with a spoonful of sour cream garnished with orange zest and mint leaves. Serves 8.

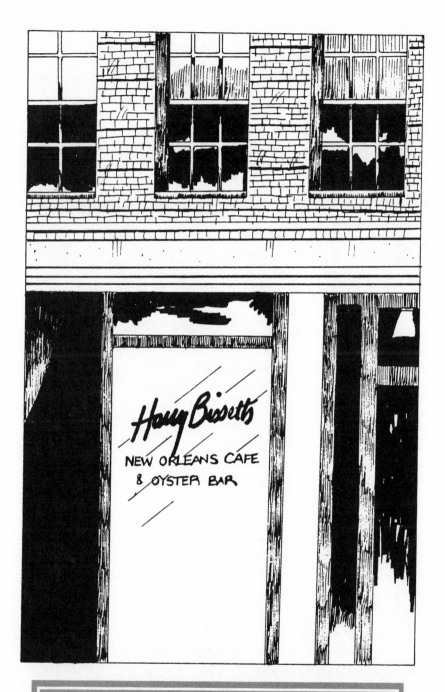

Harry Bissett's New Orleans Cafe and Oyster Bar

279 East Broad Street
ATHENS

*A*thens, Georgia, like its Mediterranean namesake, is awash in historic buildings. Both cities went in for classical columns in a big way, and both are seats of learning. Never mind if the antiquities are a tad more antique in Athens, Greece. All there is outside the Parthenon is a lemonade stand. Outside the gates of the University of Georgia is Harry Bissett's New Orleans Cafe and Oyster Bar.

Here, you can find a Fried Oyster Sandwich that will rival any you have eaten anywhere, a perfect Cajun Martini, and a Seafood Jambalaya that will warm you all the way down. And where else can you find Maque Choux? Pronounced "mock shoe," this delicious dish is a "Cajunization" of a traditional corn and tomato stew popular with the Native Americans inhabiting southern Louisiana before the Acadian migrations.

Harry Bissett's has something else, too—the style of a New Orleans restaurant. New Orleans knows something about hanging out that the rest of the world has yet to master. But Harry Bissett's comes close to capturing the secret, possibly because it is near a college known for its laid-back style. It has practically the only bar in Georgia where small children can belly up and swill a cola with their daddies without getting stared at.

Beyond the bar are tables situated upstairs and down in a courtyard covered by a skylight. For more formal dining, there is a yellow-and-green room upstairs which used to be the site of board meetings when Harry Bissett's was the University Bank of Athens. It has been meticulously and expensively restored, even to the tin ceiling, which was replaced with an authentic duplicate. Sit by a window and take a moment to look out at the Bradford pear trees and consider that only in this place have ancient Greece, old New Orleans, and a small-town Southern bank mingled their flavors in a gumbo so delightful.

Harry Bissett's Maque Choux

8 ears of corn, cleaned
½ cup coarsely chopped onion
½ cup chopped bell pepper
1 cup peeled and chopped tomatoes
   (or 1 cup canned
   stewed tomatoes)
1 teaspoon sugar
1 teaspoon black pepper
¼ teaspoon white pepper

¼ teaspoon cayenne pepper
¼ teaspoon Tabasco sauce
1 teaspoon salt
½ teaspoon thyme
½ teaspoon basil
2 whole bay leaves
½ cup chopped scallions
¼ cup chopped parsley
½ cup vegetable oil

With a sharp knife, cut the corn kernels in half lengthwise, then cut them off the cobs. Scrape the cobs with the back of the knife to remove the pulp and milk of the corn. Combine all ingredients except oil. In a large iron skillet, heat oil and add corn mixture. Be careful, as popping will occur. Lower the heat and simmer, covered, for 45 minutes, stirring occasionally. Serves 4 to 6.

Harry Bissett's Chicken Pontalba

Potato mixture

1½ sticks butter
5 potatoes, peeled and diced
½ bunch green onions, chopped
1 tablespoon minced garlic
1 pound ham, cubed
1½ cups sliced mushrooms

2 tablespoons chopped parsley
½ teaspoon salt
1 teaspoon black pepper
½ teaspoon cayenne pepper
½ teaspoon basil
1 cup white wine

In a large skillet, melt butter and sauté potatoes, onions, and garlic on low heat for 15 minutes until potatoes are browned. Add remaining ingredients and sauté another 10 minutes. Remove with a slotted spoon and keep warm while preparing sauce and chicken. Reserve liquid left in skillet.

Béarnaise Sauce

6 egg yolks
2 sticks softened butter
1/4 teaspoon salt
1/8 teaspoon cayenne pepper
1/2 tablespoon fresh lemon juice

3/4 cup Burgundy
1/2 teaspoon white vinegar
1/4 cup finely chopped shallots
2 tablespoons tarragon
1 tablespoon butter

In a double boiler, whisk egg yolks about 2 minutes over low heat. Slowly add softened butter, whisking constantly until sauce thickens. Continue whisking as you remove from heat. Add salt, pepper, and lemon juice. (This is a hollandaise sauce.) Put Burgundy, vinegar, shallots, tarragon, and 1 tablespoon butter in a small saucepan and reduce by simmering until all the liquid has evaporated. Add this mixture to the hollandaise. Keep sauce at room temperature while preparing chicken.

Chicken

1 teaspoon salt
1/4 teaspoon black pepper
1/4 teaspoon cayenne pepper
1 cup flour

4 chicken breasts,
    deboned and halved
1 cup vegetable oil

Combine seasonings and flour and dredge chicken pieces in this seasoned flour. Add oil to the reserved butter in the skillet in which the potatoes were fried and heat until butter sizzles. Fry the chicken, turning often, about 10 minutes until golden brown.

Serve in casserole or au gratin dishes with potatoes on bottom, then a layer of chicken, then lots of Béarnaise on top. Serves 4.

The Blue Willow Inn

294 North Cherokee Road S.E. (Ga.11)
(From Atlanta, take Exit 47 off I-20, turn left, and drive 2½ miles.)
SOCIAL CIRCLE

$\mathscr{M}$y children made me go to The Blue Willow Inn. They liked the name. Since my children have grown up in restaurants watching Mom scribble notes about the décor and food on the backs of napkins, they are pretty good, if ruthless, judges of restaurant character. Then, on the hour-long drive, I found that the reason they wanted to go to The Blue Willow Inn was to see a blue willow tree. I became depressed. I became even more depressed when we drove up to the inn — a stately, columned, cream-brick mansion in Social Circle — and saw a huge crowd waiting on the front porch. It was raining. My husband began sighing aloud.

Then we looked in the window and saw the buffet. There was a salad table, a soup table, a big, round dessert table covered with cakes, pies, and bowls of pudding, and, at the far end of the room, a long buffet loaded with Fried Chicken, Roast Beef, veggies, and all kinds of good things. "Shrimp!" said my daughter. "And over there, chocolate cake!" "I guess we can wait for an hour," said my husband, suddenly patient. We got a table in five minutes.

If you grew up in a small town in the South, you will feel like you've gone home when you visit this inn. It's all here — chandeliers, high ceilings with fans, big, heavy sideboards, and sweet, friendly service. But mostly, it's the food. These people are serious about traditional Southern food. They have platters of Ribs, mounds of Macaroni and Cheese, Sweet Potatoes, Peach Cobbler, soft, white Coconut Cake. They have those stubby, fat Green Beans that are only served in the South, and Fried Green Tomatoes. Eating here was a kind of personal fantasy for me. I feasted on Boiled Shrimp, Black-Eyed Peas, and Tomato Chutney and had five glasses of iced tea.

While the children were floating in the Peach Cobbler, I decided

Lunch
11:00 A.M. until 2:30 P.M.
Monday through Friday

11:00 A.M. until 3:30 P.M.
Saturday

Dinner
5:30 P.M. until 9:00 P.M.
Monday through Friday

4:30 P.M. until 9:00 P.M.
Saturday

On Sunday, the restaurant is open
11:00 A.M. until 9:00 P.M.

Reservations are recommended
for dinner, particularly on weekends
call (770) 464-2131

they needed to know the history of the inn. It was built in 1917, I told them, by cotton magnate John Upshaw for his bride, Bertha. Since the 1950s, the house had served variously as a clubhouse, a community center, and the Social Circle Church of God before Louis and Billie Van Dyke bought it in 1991 and opened The Blue Willow Inn, launching a wildly successful reincarnation. The inn is named Blue Willow for the china, not the shrubbery.

"Umm," they said. "Very interesting, Mother. Can we have another helping of dessert?"

"And Margaret Mitchell slept here."

"What? She did? In what room? How do you know?"

Well, technically, she didn't. She slept next door. Red Upshaw, a relative of the John Upshaws, was Mitchell's first husband. When they were courting, she often spent the night in the little house next door to the inn. But in Georgia, Margaret Mitchell is a name to conjure with, and one does what one can.

The Blue Willow Inn's Savannah Red Rice

2 cups uncooked rice
4 slices bacon
1 medium onion, chopped
1 small bell pepper, chopped
16-ounce can tomatoes

14-ounce bottle ketchup
1 teaspoon salt
dash of black pepper
Tabasco sauce to taste

Cook rice according to package directions. Fry bacon until crisp; drain and reserve bacon grease. Chop bacon into small pieces. Sauté onion and bell pepper in bacon grease. Combine bacon, onion, bell pepper, and remaining ingredients in an ungreased casserole and cook at 350 degrees for 40 to 50 minutes. Serves 8.

The Blue Willow Inn's Skillet Squash

6 medium yellow or
    zucchini squash
½ small onion
¼ cup butter or margarine
¼ cup water

4 slices bacon, cooked crisp and
    chopped, with grease reserved
¼ teaspoon salt
pepper to taste

Wash and slice squash. Cut onion into thin slices. In a heavy skillet, cook butter, water, onion, and 2 tablespoons bacon grease over medium heat for 4 to 5 minutes until onions are tender. Add squash, salt, and pepper; cook until squash is tender. Add chopped bacon and stir. Drain and serve. Serves 6.

The Blue Willow Inn's Creamed Corn

14-ounce can creamed corn
1 cup frozen or fresh whole-kernel
   or shoe peg corn
2 eggs
1 tablespoon self-rising flour

4 slices bacon, cooked crisp
   and chopped
1 tablespoon bacon grease
salt and pepper to taste

Combine all ingredients; mix well but do not beat. Cook in an ungreased casserole for 30 to 40 minutes at 350 degrees. Serves 6.

The Depot at Covington

4122 North Emory Street
COVINGTON

horeau hated trains. He said they were ugly, noisy, and smelly, and they frightened the animals. He may have been right, but other citizens welcomed trains because they were also fast and reliable. And exciting. By the middle of the nineteenth century, a couple could board a train to spend a few days in a faraway place and be back again in practically no time at all. A farmer could load his crops on a train and have them to market in a day, instead of the week or two it would have taken by wagon. A young teacher stuck in the wilds of western Georgia could go home to visit her folks for Christmas. The possibilities for sociability as well as commerce were infinitely increased.

11:00 A.M. until 10:00 P.M.
Monday through Thursday

11:00 A.M. until 11:00 P.M.
Friday

5:00 P.M. until 11:00 P.M.
Saturday

For reservations
call (770) 784-1128

The railroad came to Covington in 1845. The first depot, made of wood, endured hard times when General Sherman's army partially burned it and tore up the adjoining tracks in 1864. Though the depot was shortly restored to service, it was again damaged by fire in the 1880s. It was replaced in 1885 by a fine brick one which remains to this day a gathering place for people on the move. Only now it's been given new life as a restaurant. The Depot wasn't restored in a low-budget, paint-and-a-prayer fashion. From the handmade-brick walls to the wide-board floors, the building has been painstakingly and expensively brought to a luster it probably never knew in its train-station life. There are comfortable, upholstered booths here, golden oak chairs and tables, Oriental rugs, Victorian chandeliers, arched doorways with Tiffany-glass doors. A giant, shiny cappuccino machine stands at one end of the dining room. It's all as elegant as can be, in soothing green, maroon, and cream colors.

Practically as soon as you sit down, you can (and must) have Cheese Biscuits and the Bottomless Salad—a big bowl of mixed greens, tomatoes, black olives, and great dressing. As I helped myself to my third bowlful, the waitress assured me that there was more in the kitchen. By the time I finished the Shrimp Gumbo and ate a couple of my husband's Stuffed Mushrooms, I almost didn't have room for my entrée. But I managed. The New York Strip Sirloin and Fries is my favorite at The Depot. Other tasty items include Bacon-Wrapped Fillet with Shrimp, Prime Rib, Fried Fisherman's Combo, Hawaiian Chicken, Shrimp Linguine, and Chicken Chimichanga. The Cheeseburger and Fries combination is great.

You can have such a nice, relaxed meal at The Depot that you may forget you're in a train station, but try and remember as you leave to look at the train cars housing private dining rooms; they are located behind the restaurant. You might even go home whistling "Casey Jones" and dig out your old Lionel train set.

The Depot's Chicken Fettuccine

4 fresh cloves garlic, chopped
1 cup clarified butter, melted
4 cups clam juice
2 teaspoons chopped parsley
salt to taste
1 teaspoon pepper
1 teaspoon oregano

4 cups minced clams
12 ounces fettuccine noodles
1½ pounds chicken breasts,
*   skinned and deboned*
salt and pepper to taste
½ cup clarified butter
1¼ cups heavy cream

In a skillet, sauté garlic in 1 cup butter until lightly browned. Gradually add clam juice and stir in parsley, salt, pepper, and oregano. Add clams and cook until heated through. Set sauce aside. Begin cooking noodles according to package directions. While fettuccine is cooking, slice chicken into strips, add salt and pepper, and sauté in ½ cup butter until light golden and just done. Over low heat, stir in clam sauce and cream; do not boil. When noodles are done, drain them, rinse with hot water, and drain again. Then toss noodles with the chicken mixture over low heat until noodles are warmed. Serves 2 to 4.

The Depot's Sole Oscar

18 spears (approximately
*   1 pound) asparagus*
6 6-ounce sole fillets
salt and pepper to taste
flour for coating

3 eggs, slightly beaten
4 tablespoons clarified butter
9 ounces snow or lump crabmeat
1½ cups hollandaise sauce
*   (see index)*

Cook asparagus in water until just tender; do not overcook. Drain and set spears aside. Season fillets with salt and pepper and dip them in flour to coat lightly, then into eggs to cover completely. Place some of the butter in a medium-hot pan and sauté fillets for 40 seconds on each side until light golden brown and just done. Remove pan from heat. In another pan, sauté crabmeat in a little of the butter just to heat through. Sauté asparagus in a third pan in the last of the butter. Place 3 asparagus spears on each fillet and top with crabmeat. Cover with hollandaise and serve. Serves 6.

Victorian Tea Room

Main Street
WARM SPRINGS

In the 1920s, Warm Springs was a sleepy little resort town sitting on the railroad tracks in the middle of western Georgia. Folks came to stay at the Meriweather Hotel and bathe at the springs, hoping to cure what ailed them or at least pass the time pleasantly. Among the hopefuls was a young New York lawyer who had been cruelly stricken with polio in 1921 and could not seem to recover either the use of his legs or his zest for life. After his visit to the springs, the man was so impressed with his improvement that he bought the hotel and started a hospital. Then he went home and became governor of New York and, in 1932, president of the United States. Franklin Delano Roosevelt and Warm Springs thus established the mutually beneficial association that was to continue until Roosevelt's death here in 1945. Throughout his tenure as a four-term president, Roosevelt periodically retreated to his home in Warm Springs for rejuvenation.

Lunch
11:30 A.M. until 2:00 P.M.
Daily

Dinner is not served to the public, but dinner arrangements can be made for private parties.

For reservations (recommended for large groups) call (706) 655-2319

Now, Warm Springs itself is undergoing a kind of rejuvenation, as the cars and tour buses roll in on their way to the Little White House and Callaway Gardens. The village, which after Roosevelt's death became a virtual ghost town, is now a thriving tourist mecca filled with an assortment of shops offering antiques, crafts, and memorabilia. And when one tires of sightseeing, there is the Victorian Tea Room, built in 1906 as Talbot's General Mercantile. I could find no evidence that Franklin or Eleanor ever wandered into the mercantile to buy a paper and chat with the locals, but I imagine they did, and you are welcome to the same fantasy if it pleases you.

You won't need a fantasy to spice up your lunch, because the food here is plenty good enough to stand on its own. The Victorian Tea Room seats over two hundred guests and offers a daily buffet as well as a tantalizing menu.

Don't be deceived, as I was, by the *Victorian* and *Tea* portions of the restaurant's name. For me, that phraseology always connotes an abundance of discomfort and very little to eat. Happily, such is not the case here.The Tea Room is a two-story restaurant with a mezzanine that circles the main dining room. The original tongue-and-groove ceiling, which stretches twenty feet above diners, gives the place a spacious feel. The décor is hunter green, the wall covering a dusky gold damask. Lots of interesting antiques grace the walls to entertain you while you eat. Further entertainment is provided by a player grand piano, which performs during lunch; a real person plays on Sundays. The whole effect is nicely, elegantly Victorian, yet tourists wearing shorts can stop in after a visit to Roosevelt's Little White House—a mere five minutes away—and feel right at home. It's that kind of place.

Victorian Tea Room's Seafood Broccoli Casserole

*10-ounce package frozen
  broccoli spears
1 pound raw shrimp,
  peeled and deveined
  (crabmeat, sealegs, or fish
  may be substituted)*

*1 can cream of shrimp soup
1 cup mayonnaise
1 tablespoon lemon juice
1 tablespoon margarine
½ cup grated cheddar cheese
dash of paprika*

Prepare broccoli by boiling it according to package directions in salted water until tender. Drain it and lay the stalks in a shallow casserole. Top with shrimp or other seafood. Prepare a sauce by mixing soup, mayonnaise, lemon juice, margarine, and cheese in a saucepan; reserve some cheese for topping. Stir over low heat until cheese and margarine melt. If sauce seems too thick, dilute it with a little warm water. Pour sauce over seafood and broccoli; sprinkle with the leftover cheese and paprika. Bake at 350 degrees for 20 to 30 minutes until shrimp turn pink. Serves 4.

Victorian Tea Room's Squash Casserole

*6 to 8 medium yellow squash
1 medium onion
2 beaten eggs
3 tablespoons margarine
2 tablespoons pimientos
½ bell pepper, chopped*

*1 cup mayonnaise
cayenne pepper to taste
salt to taste
1¼ cups mild cheddar cheese,
  grated*

Slice squash and chop onion; simmer them together with a little water for 10 to 15 minutes until tender. Drain excess water and stir in remaining ingredients, reserving ¼ cup of cheese. Pour the mixture into a greased casserole, sprinkle with the reserved cheese, and bake at 350 degrees for 20 minutes until firm. Serves 6.

Oak Tree Victorian Dinner Restaurant

U.S. 27

HAMILTON

I arrived at Oak Tree Victorian Dinner Restaurant at dusk and found it all lit up like somebody was having a party. Oak Tree is a big, white country-Victorian house with all the requisite cupolas and shutters, so I figured the restaurant probably served country-style fare. Inside, I found a series of pastel rooms, all with twelve-foot

ceilings and Italian-marble fireplaces. An enormous copper cappuccino machine occupies the front hall. When I saw it, I began to suspect that this was not a fried-chicken emporium. When I spotted the businesslike rows of wine bottles behind it, and the uniformed bartender standing in front of enough gleaming glass to stock Macy's on a sale day, my suspicions deepened. And when I sat down and looked at the menu, I knew for sure. These people take food very seriously indeed. I was about to enjoy classic continental cuisine, so I checked my wallet surreptitiously to make sure I had my charge cards, and then I leaned back and enjoyed it.

My husband chose Medallions of Veal with Shrimp, Scallops, and Lobster Sauce and murmured sweet nothings to his plate for the rest of the meal. I had Escargots and Quail, being a purist. The Quail arrived looking like a tiny chicken, as I knew it would, and I settled down to the tedious but worthwhile task of extracting a meal from it when, lo and behold, it turned out to be deboned and stuffed, then cunningly reassembled to look like its former self. Those of you who order quail all the time no doubt expect that sort of trouble to be taken on your behalf. I, who grew up eating buckshot quail, was bowled over. The thing was so beautiful I was reluctant to eat it, but gluttony overcame art.

Good French restaurants affect people that way. There should be a moment of hesitation and wonderment—"All this for me?"—before you dive in. And there should be a little frivolity, a little surprise, like the one that awaits you when you slice open Oak Tree's Chicken Duxelle. Or the delight inherent in inverting your first homemade bowlful of Crème Caramel and watching that honey-colored sauce envelop the custard. French cooking is a kind of magic, and Oak Tree Victorian Dinner Restaurant has an inordinate number of rabbits in its hat.

Oak Tree Victorian Dinner Restaurant's Chicken Duxelle

4 4-ounce chicken breasts,
   deboned and skinned
salt and white pepper to taste
1 medium onion, diced fine
4 shallot bulbs, diced fine
2 cloves garlic, diced fine
2 tablespoons butter
2 cups fresh mushrooms, chopped

½ ounce good brandy
2 cups fresh breadcrumbs
½ cup chopped parsley
½ cup seasoned flour
1 egg
½ cup water
1 cup chopped pecans

Pound chicken breasts between sheets of plastic wrap until they are very thin, like a lace curtain. Season lightly with salt and white pepper and refrigerate at least 1 hour.

To make the duxelle, sauté onions, shallots, and garlic in butter until golden. Add mushrooms. Cook until moisture evaporates and the mixture is light brown. Add brandy and cook to evaporate the alcohol. Add just enough breadcrumbs to tighten the mixture to a paste. Add parsley. Spread the mushroom paste on the glossy side of each chicken breast and roll it up jelly-roll fashion, folding in the edges. Refrigerate again for 1 hour or longer.

Roll each breast in seasoned flour. Blend the egg and water, then dip chicken in the egg wash and roll it in a mixture of pecans and the remaining breadcrumbs. Fry in 375-degree deep fat 1 or 2 minutes until golden. Arrange the breasts in a casserole and bake at 375 degrees for 25 minutes. Serves 4.

Oak Tree Victorian Dinner Restaurant's Creme Caramel

Caramel

2 tablespoons butter
1 cup sugar

⅓ cup water

Lightly grease 10 custard cups with melted butter. Melt the sugar in water in a small pan and cook over low heat until amber colored. Coat the custard cups with the mixture, using approximately 1 tablespoon per cup.

Custard

3 eggs

8 egg yolks

4 cups milk

½ cup sugar

1 teaspoon vanilla extract

pinch of salt

Preheat oven to 300 degrees. Beat the eggs and yolks with a mixer or whisk until creamy. Scald the milk (do not boil) and add it to the eggs. Add sugar, vanilla, and salt. Pour 6 ounces of custard into each cup and set the cups in a pan, adding water to the pan to make a water bath for the custard. Bake approximately 1½ hours until set.

To serve, run a knife around the edge of the custard and invert it onto a plate. Serves 10.

The Farmhouse

469 Farmhouse Road
ELLERSLIE

The first time I saw The Farmhouse, there was a line of people standing patiently outside, waiting to eat lunch. Since the restaurant is several miles from anywhere and down a country road at that, I was intrigued and sauntered over to the end of the line to wait with them. There was a half-acre of flatbed trucks and Cadillac, Mercedes, and Volkswagen automobiles parked

in the yard—like a wake. No one was sad, though, or even surly. Everyone was laughing and talking and have a good time. No one looked at his watch.

"This place must be really something," I ventured.

"Well . . . we like it."

"What's good to eat?"

"Oh, everything. Everything is quite good."

Once inside, I discovered that, though The Farmhouse is clean and rustic, no effort has been made to preserve the house for its own sake. Nobody famous ever lived there, and it's not architecturally important, except perhaps in one significant respect—its very ordinariness. The house was built around 1900 for tenants or sharecroppers, and it is typical of the plain, no-frills life they led.

When my food arrived, I found that it, too, was ordinary, and I finally knew why everyone in the line had been grinning. Lunch was wonderful. Not pig-out wonderful, like an all-you-can-eat place. Not greasy wonderful, like a fish house. Not elegantly wonderful, like an uptown dining spot. Just plain, ordinary good. There was the perfect Meat Loaf, a delicious Squash Casserole, mouth-watering Sour Cream Cornbread, the Coconut Cake I'd been looking for all my life. All the delectable cakes—Caramel Layer Cake, Brown Sugar Cake, Lemon-Pineapple Layer Cake—will test a dieter's resolve.

"We started this place sixteen years ago as an outlet for our crafts," said the owners. "We had two tables, and we brought Mom out here to cook for us. It just grew. Now, we serve two or three hundred people a weekend." The mom referred to is Katie Osborne, and she makes all the food herself. It's no wonder the lines are so long.

The Farmhouse's Coconut Cake

Cake

1 cup unsalted butter

2 cups sugar

4 eggs

½ teaspoon salt

1 tablespoon vanilla

1 teaspoon soda

1½ cups buttermilk

3 cups plain flour

Cream the butter and sugar. Add unbeaten eggs 1 at a time, beating with a mixer after each addition. Add salt and vanilla. Stir soda into buttermilk. To the first mixture, add about ½ cup flour, then some of the buttermilk, beating after each addition. Continue adding the ingredients, alternating until the buttermilk and flour are gone. Grease three 8-inch cake pans and cut wax paper to fit the bottoms. Divide the batter among the pans, shake it down, and bake at 350 degrees for 20 minutes until cake tests done. Cool the layers for 10 minutes and then remove them from the pans, leaving the wax paper stuck to the cake. Stack the layers on top of each other and cover with a light towel overnight or until completely cold. Then take the layers apart, removing the wax paper and rolling with fingers any brown particles remaining on the cake, so there is no crust on the tops of the layers.

Frosting

3 cups sugar

1½ cups milk

2 9-ounce packages frozen coconut, defrosted

1 stick unsalted butter

1 teaspoon vanilla

Cook the sugar and milk together until liquid begins to boil; cook another 10 minutes. Add coconut and reduce heat. Continue cooking slowly until mixture changes color slightly, from white to oyster white. Remove from heat, add butter and vanilla, and stir well.

Let frosting cool to lukewarm and spread it between the layers and on top of cake; it will seep down into the cake and make it very moist and good. Store in the refrigerator for 1 or 2 days before eating. Yields 1 cake.

The Farmhouse's Stir-Fry Cabbage

½ cabbage
1 small onion
1 bell pepper
2 stalks celery
2 fresh tomatoes

salt and pepper to taste
½ to 1 teaspoon sugar
1 tablespoon oil
1 tablespoon butter or margarine

Chop cabbage into strips and cut up onion, bell pepper, and celery. Peel and chop tomatoes. Sprinkle the vegetables with salt and pepper and sugar. Heat the oil and butter in a large frying pan or wok and add the vegetables, cooking for 2 minutes. Then cook for 2 more minutes with the lid on. Serves 6.

The Farmhouse's Sour Cream Cornbread

1½ cups self-rising cornmeal
2 tablespoons sugar
2 eggs
½ cup cooking oil

1 cup cream-style corn,
  fresh or frozen
1 medium onion, chopped
1 cup sour cream

Mix all ingredients well. Grease large muffin tins and pour them about ¾ full of batter. Bake at 400 degrees for 20 to 25 minutes. Serve hot. Yields 16 to 18 muffins.

Bludau's Goétchius House

405 Broadway
COLUMBUS

$\mathcal{G}$o to Bludau's Goétchius House expecting knockwurst and beer and you will be disappointed. Richard Rose Goétchius, who built his house in 1834, was a New Yorker who came south and adopted Southern ways to the extent of building this New Orleans–style mansion for his bride. It now sits on the banks of the Chattahoochee River at the end of a row of staunch Federal cottages

Dinner
5:00 P.M. until 9:45 P.M.
Monday through Thursday

5:00 P.M. until 10:45 P.M.
Friday and Saturday

For reservations
(strongly recommended)
call (706) 324-4863

like an exuberant wild rose sprouting in a tulip bed. It looks quite natural here but in truth was chopped into seven pieces and relocated on the spot some thirty years ago.

While you dine, you can entertain yourself wondering where the mansion was cut and how the people who cut it ever put it back together. It's an enormous, wandering place, with many little dining rooms leading into other dining rooms. Downstairs is a dark, wonderful bar. Outside is a patio with a fountain. You can even eat on the back porch if you like. The décor is "New Orleans Victorian," with gold curtains and lots of roses in the carpets. The menu is large and varied.

A typical dinner might begin with an hors d'oeuvres sampler—Oysters Rockefeller, Clams Casino, Escargots Duxelles, Frog Legs Bourguignonne, and Stuffed Mushrooms. In fact, it might end there, and quite happily, but then you'd miss getting to choose among fresh Red Snapper Française, Chicken Terrine with Pâté, Steak Diane, Rack of Lamb, and Rack of Veal. To finish, try the Bananas Foster. Or pick a wedge from the cake cart. I picked three wedges, amazing my friends and relations, and fought my son for the last bite of Lemon Cake. He won, being only three and not averse to screaming to make a point.

The most pleasant thing about Bludau's Goétchius House besides the food and the house itself is the feeling that if your three-year-old son did decide to throw a massive fit in the middle of dinner, no one would care. A waiter would probably come over and make faces at him until he forgot to be unhappy. In case you don't have children, let me explain. There are many restaurants serving good food, many historic restaurants, and many restaurants tolerant of children, but all three qualities are rarely found in the *same* restaurant. Bludau's Goétchius House is such a restaurant.

Bludau's Goétchius House's Garlic Butter

small bunch of scallions
¼ cup Burgundy
2 sticks butter
2 sticks margarine
1 teaspoon ground cloves

½ onion, chopped
2 cloves garlic, minced
¼ cup fresh parsley, chopped
¼ cup shallots

Chop the scallions and boil them in Burgundy until the Burgundy is evaporated. In a food processor, whip the butter and margarine. Add the other ingredients and process until very fluffy. Yields 2¼ cups.

Note: Garlic Butter can be frozen in tablespoon-size lumps and added to any sautéed fish.

Bludau's Goétchius House's Veal Naturel

1-pound veal tenderloin,
  hand-sliced
dash of thyme
dash of lemon juice
salt and pepper to taste
flour for dredging

2 tablespoons butter
2 tablespoons oil
½ pound mushrooms, sliced
10 scallions, chopped
¼ to ½ cup cream sherry
rissolé potatoes (optional)

Sprinkle veal slices with thyme, lemon juice, and salt and pepper and marinate for several hours in the refrigerator. Flour the pieces lightly and sauté a few at a time in butter and oil until brown. Remove veal from pan and keep warm. Add more butter to the pan if needed and sauté mushrooms and scallions until glazed. Then add cream sherry, cover the pan, and simmer for a minute. Pour sauce over veal and, if desired, serve with rissolé potatoes. Serves 2 to 4.

Bludau's Goétchius House's Red Snapper Française

1 fresh snapper, filleted
salt and pepper to taste
¼ teaspoon thyme
¼ teaspoon Hungarian paprika
1 egg
1 teaspoon fresh parsley, minced
½ teaspoon mixed Parmesan
  and Romano cheeses

1 tablespoon butter
1 tablespoon oil
flour for dredging
1 tablespoon Garlic Butter
  (recipe above)
splash of sherry

Cut fish into 3 or so pieces and season with salt and pepper, thyme, and paprika. In a shallow bowl, stir together egg, parsley, and cheese. In a frying pan, melt butter with oil on medium-low heat until hot. Coat the fish pieces with flour and dip them into the egg mix, then place in the frying pan. Sauté until golden brown on the bottom, then turn them over and add Garlic Butter and sherry to the pan. Sauté until done and serve immediately. Serves 1 to 2.

The Rankin Quarter

21 East 10th Street
(2 blocks north of the restoration area)
COLUMBUS

$\mathcal{B}$ack in the 1880s, when Columbus was a busy river port, The Rankin Hotel was, I imagine, a handy place for travelers to spend the night before boarding a steamboat south to the Gulf of Mexico. It was large, square, and brick, and it stood a convenient two blocks from the Chattahoochee, providing a bed and victuals to all passersby. It also had the distinction of being the first hotel in town with indoor bathrooms. Bathrooms are of course commonplace now, and a bed at The Rankin is no longer a possibility, but the old place is once again feeding people in style and comfort.

Lunch
11:00 A.M. until 2:30 P.M.
Sunday through Friday

Dinner
Served on nights
when the Springer Opera House
is hosting performances.

Reservations are not
necessary, but the phone number
is (706) 322-8151

The downstairs, which once housed a newsstand and a grocery store, has been stripped down to the original brick. The windows are wide, curving arches, some of which look out upon an interior courtyard. It's a comfortable, airy, no-nonsense sort of place where lots of different types of people feel at home. Business people can get a quick bite and talk over a deal or linger by the lovely Victorian bar and sip a libation. Couples and tourists can relax over conversation or maps. Tired mothers can take a table along the banquette which runs down one wall and prop their babies beside them as they eat.

During my last visit, I sat in a corner and watched just such an assortment rush in, along with about two hundred of their friends. They were all served and happily eating in about fifteen minutes. The staff here believes in giving people value for their money. Parading by my table were steaming soups, fresh-looking salads, luscious sandwiches, and plates and plates of Lasagna, the special that day. The menu features deli fare—including a "Create Your Own" sandwich—and daily specials announced on a chalkboard in the foyer.

Harry McMahan, who bought the restaurant in 1989, has continued the tradition of hospitality established in the 1800s and has expanded the business to include catering both on and off the premises. The restaurant has catered parties for as many as fourteen hundred guests, and in such varied locations as a riverboat and the Springer

Opera House. The citizens of Columbus are certainly fortunate to have such an establishment.

The Rankin Quarter's Banana Fluff

Crust

1 cup self-rising flour
½ cup chopped pecans

1 stick butter, melted

Combine ingredients and press into an 8½-by-11-inch baking dish. Bake in a preheated 350-degree oven for 20 minutes. Let cool.

Filling

8 ounces soft cream cheese
½ cup confectioners' sugar
7 ounces instant vanilla
   pudding mix

2 cups milk
8 ounces commercial
   whipped topping
2 bananas, sliced

In a large bowl, cream with a mixer the cream cheese and sugar. Add pudding mix, milk, and whipped topping; beat well.

Place a layer of sliced bananas on the crust and top with the pudding mixture. Cover and refrigerate overnight. Serves 6 to 8.

The Rankin Quarter's Ham Delite

1 cup fresh mushrooms, sliced
1 small onion, chopped
2 tablespoons butter
2 tablespoons cooking sherry
1 English muffin

1 tablespoon mayonnaise
3 ounces sliced ham
2 slices tomato
2 slices Swiss cheese

Sauté mushrooms and onions in butter and sherry over low heat for 15 to 20 minutes. Remove from heat. Split muffin and spread each side with mayonnaise. Pile on ham and top with sautéed vegetables, tomato slices, and cheese. Heat in a 400-degree oven or in a microwave (for 1½ minutes on high) until cheese melts. Serves 1.

The Rankin Quarter's Grammy's Baked Beans

¼ pound bacon, chopped
1 medium onion, chopped
2-pound can pork and beans
½ cup light brown sugar
½ teaspoon liquid smoke

1 tablespoon Worcestershire sauce
2 tablespoons Gulden's mustard
2 tablespoons ketchup
2 tablespoons sweet-pickle cubes
1½ tablespoons light corn syrup

Brown bacon and onion in a frying pan. Combine remaining ingredients in a baking pan. Add the bacon and onion and bake at 350 degrees for 1 to 1½ hours. Serves 10 to 12.

The Left Banque

On the Square on Johnston Street
FORSYTH

In 1908, you could have stood on the square in Forsyth on a Saturday morning and seen much the same thing you see now. The Monroe County Courthouse sat smack in the middle of the square, a proud testament to the county's progressive outlook. On the courthouse lawn, the obligatory Confederate monument had just been unveiled. The place would have been bustling with folks coming to town to do business at the cotton exchange or the brokerage office or spending their money at one of the stores lining the square. There were no sidewalks then, and you might have had to pick your way around bales of cotton awaiting shipment and teams and wagons parked haphazardly along the road. As you sauntered along Johnston Street, you would have remembered that Joel Chandler Harris used to sit and compose stories in a building on the corner. On the next corner was the town's newest bank, with Forsyth Mercantile conveniently next door. The mercantile was partitioned and had separate entrances for men and women—on the theory, presumably, that members of either sex would rather shop for their BVD's or corsets in comparative privacy.

Now, the cotton bales and horses are gone, but the mercantile and bank are still here, having been transformed into a bar and restaurant called The Left Banque, with an adjoining series of snappy little shops. You can come here and reminisce over lunch. A cafe bar facing the street offers an opportunity for more spontaneous thirst-quenching as well.

The building's restorers have kept, wherever possible, the wide-plank flooring and decorative motifs which originally characterized the place, adding such touches as murals, a carousel horse, antique leaded windows from England, and, quite curiously, lampposts from Macon's old Second Street Bridge. It's a perfect lunch layover if you're traveling I-75. As a bonus, you can sample the Cream of Broccoli Soup, which is the best I've ever tested or ever hope to taste. The

Lunch
11:30 A.M. until 2:30 P.M.
Monday through Saturday

Dinner
5:00 P.M. until 9:30 P.M.
Monday through Saturday

For reservations
call (912) 994-3383

Mandarin Orange Salad is also a knockout, and I've included both recipes for you.

The Left Banque's Cream of Broccoli Soup

4 cups chicken broth
10-ounce package frozen
   chopped broccoli
2 medium onions, chopped
1 stick butter

½ cup flour
4 cups milk
½ cup cream or half-and-half
salt and pepper to taste

In a medium saucepan, heat chicken broth and add broccoli and onions. Simmer uncovered for 20 to 30 minutes while preparing the rest of the soup. In a small sauté pan, melt butter and add flour, stirring over low heat for 3 or 4 minutes to make a roux; let cool to room temperature. Heat the milk in a large saucepan and add the cooled roux, stirring with a whisk for 4 or 5 minutes; the mixture will be quite thick. When the broccoli-onion broth is ready, stir it gradually into the thickened milk. If soup seems to be getting too thin, reserve some of the broth. Add cream or half-and-half and season with salt and pepper. Serves 4 to 6.

The Left Banque's Soy Sauce Dressing

¼ cup water
½ cup soy sauce
3 tablespoons sugar

3 tablespoons vinegar
½ teaspoon garlic salt
½ cup oil

Mix all ingredients together and store in refrigerator. Use on spinach salad. Yields approximately 2 cups.

The Left Banque's Mandarin Orange Salad

Dressing

¼ cup orange juice concentrate
¼ cup sugar
3 tablespoons lemon juice

3 tablespoons sweet vermouth
3 tablespoons vinegar
¾ cup oil

Mix all ingredients well. This dressing is good on any fruit salad and may be stored in the refrigerator.

Salad

4 large lettuce leaves
4 cups mandarin orange segments

4 tablespoons toasted
almond slivers

To serve, place a lettuce leaf on each of 4 plates and cover with a mound of mandarin orange segments and a sprinkle of toasted almond slivers. Cover with dressing. Serves 4.

Whistle Stop Cafe

McCracken Street (Route 1)
(Take exit 61 off I-75 and follow signs for Juliette;
the restaurant is about 8 miles off the interstate.)
JULIETTE

Some people travel to Juliette, Georgia, to see the Whistle Stop Cafe because *Fried Green Tomatoes* was filmed here and they can buy a T-shirt that says so. Some people come for a rural-experience thing, to listen to the train and so on. Some come to see the Ocmulgee River. Some, like me, come for the food.

First, the history: in the beginning was the Ocmulgee River, then in 1882 came the railroad, then came the little town of Juliette. The town grew up around the railroad, which split it and gave it its name and reputation. It was named by a railroad engineer for his daughter, Juliette McCracken. The town soon boasted a big gristmill, a cotton mill, churches, and a school. In 1907, it got a one-lane bridge, the only bridge over the Ocmulgee for many miles. It cost a nickel to walk across it and a dime to drive a wagon or a car.

In 1927, Edward Williams built a general mercantile store here, a white clapboard building that sat right by the railroad tracks. He and his wife and six children supplied the citizens of Juliette with everything they needed to live. Groceries could be charged and also delivered. Now, antique reminders of Mr. Williams's store still decorate the place in its current incarnation. The meat block and scales, an old safe, and a wood stove are among the interesting reminders of a storekeeping past.

For forty-five years, Mr. Willliams kept the store. Then he quit. "I have had enough," he said. At that time, Juliette was at a low point; the mills had both closed and the little town was dying.

Then, in 1991, like a Hollywood movie came—well, a Hollywood movie. The gods of cinema saw little Juliette and they were well pleased. It would make a perfect setting, they felt, for *Fried Green Tomatoes*. And so it did. Juliette became Whistle Stop, a small Alabama town, and the mercantile store became the Whistle Stop Cafe. The rest, as they say, is cinematic history.

Kathy Bates and Jessica Tandy are long gone now, but the Whistle Stop Cafe is still here, still partly owned by the Williams family, still serving Fried Green Tomatoes. It is marvelously authentic. It isn't *like* a period-piece cafe, it *is* a period-piece cafe—wooden booths, white wooden walls decorated with old signs, and a big wraparound counter in the middle with stools. Ceiling fans stir the air. You can look at pictures of movie stars or the flood of 1994, when the Ocmulgee rose thirty-two feet above the levee and drowned the town, leaving tons of mud in the Whistle Stop and other businesses when the waters receded. Mostly, though, you can sit in one of the booths and eat Fried Green Tomatoes. Yes, they are served for both breakfast and lunch.

The food at the Whistle Stop is simple. Fried foods are prepared in a health-conscious oil low in saturated fat. Breakfast includes normal Southern fare—Pancakes, Eggs, Bacon, Grits, Country Ham, and so on. The lunch menu changes daily. It typically features Hamburgers, Hot Dogs, sandwiches, and a lunch plate—a choice of three meats, like Barbecued Ribs and Lemon Pepper Chicken, and assorted vegetables, like Field Peas, Collard Greens, Red Potatoes, Gumbo, Cucumber Salad—and Fried Green Tomatoes.

I'll not kid you. If you use the recipe before you, your Fried Green Tomatoes won't be as good as the originals at the Whistle Stop. Perhaps there's a knack. It is possible, however, to approximate. We must not quibble, mustn't wallow in memories. Make up a pitcher of iced tea and a plateful of Fried Green Tomatoes, plug in the movie, and have an excellent two hours. But you really owe it to yourself to go to Juliette someday and do the real thing.

Whistle Stop Cafe's Fried Green Tomatoes

2 medium green tomatoes
½ teaspoon salt
½ teaspoon pepper

½ cup white cornmeal
¼ cup bacon drippings

Cut tomatoes into ¼-inch slices and sprinkle them with salt and pepper. Dredge them in cornmeal. Heat bacon drippings in a heavy skillet, add tomatoes, and cook over medium heat until light brown, turning once. Serves 2 to 3.

Whistle Stop Cafe's Cucumber Salad

2 medium cucumbers
1 medium onion
4 red tomatoes
2 raw yellow squash

1 zucchini (optional)
1 cup apple cider vinegar
1 cup water

Peel cucumbers in stripes, leaving on half the peel. Peel onion. Chop all the vegetables into bite-size chunks and place them in a plastic container. Add vinegar and water and stir; add more vinegar and water in equal measure if needed to cover vegetables completely. Marinate for 8 hours in the refrigerator. To serve, remove the vegetables with a slotted spoon and place in small dishes. The vinegar-water mixture may be reused. Serves 4 to 6.

Beall's 1860

315 College Street
MACON

In the eighteenth century, English settlers stuck mostly to coastal Georgia, where they grew rice and fought Spaniards, mosquitoes, and gnats in great numbers. The settlers ventured upriver to the fall line but couldn't navigate around the rapids that marked all the rivers at

that elevation. By the nineteenth century, however, those rapids became useful as a source of power, and Macon—along with Augusta, Milledgeville, and Columbus—became an industrial and commercial center. Tradesmen and planters flowed in, and cotton became king of the South.

Not only was cotton king, but wealthy planters like Nathan Beall built homes fit for a king. During the 1850s, Beall was bringing cotton from his Jones County plantation into Macon to be shipped via the Ocmulgee River to Savannah. He became so enchanted by Macon's social life that he decided to build a home there. It took Beall from 1855 to 1860 to complete his fashionable Italian Renaissance home—atrocious timing, as it turned out, since Union forces occupied Macon four years later. When his Jones County plantation was destroyed, Beall was forced to sell his town house to the Stevens family.

A few years later, the house was sold again, this time to the Jordan family. The first Mrs. Jordan took great pride in running her new home with style. In fact, she felt such attachment that in the years following her death, her spirit often materialized at the top of the stairs. That was not exactly the reception Mr. Jordan had planned for his second wife, who soon spotted the first Mrs. Jordan.

In the 1900s, the new owner, Judge Dunlap, made extensive structural changes by removing the cupola and rounded roof and adding tin columns to three sides, transforming the facade to Greek Revival. He also stuccoed the exterior and created the two-story vaulted foyer, which makes an impressive entrance. The Lassiters bought the house in 1939. After her husband's death a year later, Mrs. Lassiter turned the family home into a boardinghouse. Her elegant buffet and garden parties were renowned until her retirement in the 1960s.

Today, the old house is once again serving the citizens of Macon in style and splendor. A recent renovation has given the whole place a light and airy feeling. The barrel-vaulted main dining room is impressive, as is the food. Beall's offers a variety of seafood, steak, and chicken dishes and is known for its Chicken Sweet and Hot, which is served with a slightly sweet sauce that has overtones of a spicy barbecue sauce. In my eternal quest for quick but elegant-looking company food, I was impressed with the Tournedos of Beef, which can be grilled and the sauce stirred together in a few minutes by two hungry folk, and the Poached Salmon with Fresh Fruit, which makes a great, different summer entrée.

Since the spirit of the first Mrs. Jordan has not been seen or heard from in some time, I assume that she is well pleased with the tasty adaptation of her stately home. I certainly am.

Beall's Tournedos of Beef

4 3-ounce medallions
  of beef tenderloin
4 tablespoons olive oil
salt and pepper to taste
8 ounces demi-glace or
  peppercorn sauce
  (Knorr Classic Sauces)

4 ounces Burgundy
12 fresh mushrooms, sliced
12 scallions, sliced

Coat medallions with olive oil and place them on a grill; season with salt and pepper and grill to desired doneness. While the steaks are grilling, place demi-glace or peppercorn sauce, Burgundy, mushrooms, and scallions into a sauté pan and cook until reduced by ¼. Place steaks on a plate and spoon sauce over them. Serves 2 to 4.

Beall's Poached Salmon with Fresh Fruit

2 cups water
3 cups pineapple juice
salt and pepper to taste
1 sprig fresh dill
4 6-ounce salmon fillets
  or steaks, skinless
1 kiwi, peeled

10 to 12 strawberries, hulled
¼ cantaloupe, peeled and seeded
¼ pineapple, peeled and cored
1 tablespoon red wine vinegar
½ tablespoon Tabasco sauce
1 tablespoon sugar

Combine water, pineapple juice, salt and pepper, and dill and bring to a slow boil in a sauté pan. Add salmon fillets and poach them in the liquid for 4 to 7 minutes, depending on thickness. Check salmon with a fork to see that it has turned a light pink color throughout. Remove salmon and keep warm. Chop kiwi, strawberries, cantaloupe, and pineapple in a food processor; remove to a nonreactive bowl. Combine vinegar, Tabasco, and sugar and add to the fruit, mixing well. Place salmon on each of 4 plates and spoon fruit mixture over top. Serves 4.

P. Faires

Sassafras Tea Room

2242 Ingleside Avenue
MACON

It doesn't matter whether your childhood home looked like this one-story frame house or not; the minute you walk through the front door, you get that "coming home" feeling. This home was built in the cottage style for Preston Walker and his family. Today, the baseboards, mantel, and window frames wear a coat of purple paint—not the usual color used when this house, one of the first prefab homes of 1939, was built. But oddly enough, the purple seems to go with an old organdy apron that hangs on a wall amidst hot pads and a green crocheted dresser scarf.

Lunch
11:00 A.M. until 2:00 P.M.
Tuesday through Saturday

Reservations are
needed only for groups
call (912) 746-3336

The Sassafras Tea Room is where owner Mari Riggins serves many old favorites that your mother might have made, like homemade Chicken Pot Pie and Lemon Chess Pie. But most of the menu is made up of trendy lunch dishes like Chunky Chicken Salad, with its big, bite-size chunks of tender white chicken, pineapple, nuts, and a wisp of curry to add personality. The Spinach and Cheese Quiche that I sampled was also a pleasant selection. The restaurant's premier dessert is Almond Meringue, which permeates the taste buds. The meringue is the one recipe Riggins had to promise not to divulge when she signed the contract to buy the restaurant. But don't be disappointed, because the Chocolate Chip Pie is another winner. A confirmed chocoholic, I was thrilled to have this recipe.

At the Sassafras Tea Room, every table is set with print tablecloths from the thirties or forties that look as if they might have been on your grandmother's table. You won't see two tables set with the same china or silverware. In fact, you may feel moved to get up and walk around the other rooms, as I did, and relive your own upbringing.

In a neighboring dining room, one of the walls is adorned with what my grandmother would have called a "wash dress," and the window treatments wear a creative collage of tatted and crocheted doilies and scarves.

In a breezeway, you'll see shelves filled with sets of glasses from the forties and fifties and an antique dresser set with an oil lamp and old vinegar pitchers.

Outside, a handsome oak tree spreads its strong limbs over the glassed-in front porch, which makes it hard to leave a restaurant that can resurrect such good memories and serve wholesome and delicious food at the same time.

Sassafras Tea Room's Chunky Chicken Salad

5 cups cooked chicken, diced
1 cup chopped celery
7-ounce can crushed pineapple
½ of a 7-ounce can of
    water chestnuts, drained
    and chopped

1 cup mayonnaise
¾ teaspoon curry powder
1 tablespoon soy sauce
1 tablespoon lemon juice

Combine chicken, celery, pineapple, and water chestnuts in a medium bowl. In a small bowl, combine mayonnaise, curry powder, soy sauce, and lemon juice until well mixed. Add to chicken mixture; cover and refrigerate. Serves 10.

Sassafras Tea Room's Chocolate Chip Pie

4 eggs
1 cup flour
1 cup granulated sugar
1 cup brown sugar
2 sticks margarine, melted

12-ounce package semisweet
    chocolate chips
1½ cups walnut or pecan pieces
1 teaspoon vanilla
2 8-inch unbaked pie shells

Beat eggs until foamy and whisk in flour, granulated sugar, brown sugar, and margarine until well combined. Add chocolate chips, nuts, and vanilla. Pour into pie shells and bake in a preheated 300- to 350-degree oven for 45 minutes. Yields 2 pies.

Sassafras Tea Room's Lemon Chess Pie

1 cup sugar
1 tablespoon cornstarch
4 eggs, beaten
¼ cup lemon juice

¼ cup melted butter or margarine
9-inch unbaked pie shell
whipped cream, strawberries,
    or other fresh fruit (optional)

Preheat oven to 350 degrees. Mix sugar and cornstarch in a large bowl, pressing out any large lumps. Beat in eggs, stir in lemon juice, and blend in butter. Pour the filling into the pie shell. Bake 35 to 45 minutes until puffed and golden brown. Cool before serving. The filling will thicken and fall, acquiring a jellylike texture as it cools. Garnish with whipped cream, strawberries, or other fresh fruit if desired. Yields 1 pie.

New Perry Hotel and Motel

800 Main Street
PERRY

There's an old saying that claims a person "can get more with honey than with vinegar." During the Civil War, the women of Perry took that adage to heart when Union troops camped near their homes. These wise ladies and their children brought buttermilk and cookies to the soldiers in their camp. However, one of the soldiers not only took the food from two young boys but their horse as well. When the boys' mother learned of their mistreatment, she gave the camp officer a vinegary tongue-lashing that resulted in the return of the horse. Overall, though, it is believed that the women's simple act of kindness saved Perry from being burned and pillaged, as were so many neighboring areas.

Breakfast
7:00 A.M. until 11:00 A.M.
Daily

Lunch
11:30 A.M. until 2:30 P.M.
Daily

Dinner
5:30 P.M. until 9:00 P.M.
Daily

For reservations
(accepted but not required)
call (912) 987-1000
or (800) 877-3779

Had the Union soldiers broken camp and ventured into Perry, they would have been comfortable at Cox's Inn, built of wood in 1850 as a stagecoach stop. Twenty-some years later, when the railroad was extended to Perry, the finer Perry Hotel was built. That building was razed in 1924, and what is now known as the New Perry Hotel was erected the following year. I arrived at this venerable establishment a little late for dinner. Owners Harold Green and daughter Marsha Green Haley could have told me that the dining room was closed and I would have understood, but instead that old Perry hospitality emerged.

An hour later, we sat in the main dining room and talked as I devoured very moist Pan-Broiled Chicken, a helping of Macaroni and Cheese, and a truly excellent Cornbread Dressing. While I was traveling through Georgia, other restaurateurs had suggested that I try New Perry's Shredded Yams and its Broccoli Casserole. The yams weren't available that evening, but the broccoli, with its rich cheese and herb dressing, was wonderfully Southern. While in the center of peach country, I wasn't about to pass up the Peach Pan Pie, and I quickly understood why people pull off the interstate year after year for a slice.

At breakfast the next morning, the Greens and I dined in the Garden Dining Room, which was filled with fresh camellias from their garden. It was a country breakfast of fresh Fruit, Country Ham, Biscuits, Sausage, Eggs, and Salt Pork. I learned that salt pork was once called "sawmill steak." This meat was popular because it was affordable for mill workers and didn't require refrigeration—quite an advantage at a time when few people owned iceboxes. Then, just when I thought I couldn't swallow another delicious bite, my hosts surprised me with a batch of Shredded Yams. They didn't want me to come so far and be disappointed, so the cook had made a fresh batch that morning. Now, that's what I mean by Perry hospitality!

New Perry Hotel's Shredded Yams

2 pounds raw sweet potatoes
1 tablespoon salt
1 cup sugar
½ cup white Karo syrup

½ cup water
¼ cup margarine
1 cup pineapple juice

Preheat oven to 350 degrees. Peel potatoes and shred them in a grinder, with the shredder in a food processor, or with a hand grater. Place in a gallon of water. Add salt. Drain and wash well. Place potatoes in an 11½-by-7½-inch buttered baking dish. In a medium saucepan, mix sugar, syrup, and ½ cup water. Cook over medium heat until mixture becomes a simple syrup. Add margarine. Pour pineapple juice over potatoes, then add syrup. Bake 35 minutes until potatoes are transparent. Serves 12.

New Perry Hotel's Peach Pan Pie

piecrust dough (favorite recipe)
1 cup sugar
¼ cup water
3 cups fresh peaches, sliced
to medium thickness

2 to 3 tablespoons butter
2 to 3 tablespoons all-purpose flour

Set aside half of pie dough in refrigerator. Roll out remaining half in a circle. Fit dough into bottom of an 8-inch pie plate and prick bottom with a fork. In a medium saucepan, combine sugar and water and bring to a boil for a few seconds. Add peaches and simmer for about 10 minutes. Place a layer of peaches in bottom of piecrust, dot with cubes of butter, and sprinkle evenly with flour. Repeat procedure until all peaches are used. Roll out remaining piecrust and place over top of peaches, crimping sides with a fork to seal. Cut slits in top of pie. Bake in a preheated 350-degree oven for 30 to 40 minutes until crust is light brown. Yields 1 pie.

New Perry Hotel's Broccoli Casserole

2 10-ounce packages
  frozen broccoli
3 to 4 tablespoons butter
1 cup herb-flavored stuffing
  (commercial)

1 can cream of mushroom soup
1 cup grated cheddar cheese
¼ cup milk
1 teaspoon grated onions
dash of salt

Preheat oven to 350 degrees. Cook broccoli according to package directions and drain. Butter a 1½- to 2-quart casserole dish. In a mixing bowl, combine all ingredients, then spread evenly in casserole. Bake for 30 minutes. Serves 6.

Windsor Hotel

125 West Lamar Street
AMERICUS

The Windsor is jokingly described as "a restaurant with a lot of rooms attached." But when its 1892 exterior is lit with six thousand tiny white lights, it takes on the look of a fairy-tale castle. The hotel's Romanesque architecture, designed by Gottfried L. Norman, is replete with turrets, a Flemish stepped roof, and other distinctions. This grande dame, now on the National Register of Historic Places, was completely rehabilitated through a grass-roots effort that cost $5.8 million in 1991. It is heartwarming to learn that Mayor Russell Thomas, Jr.,

Breakfast
7:30 A.M. until 10:30 A.M.
Daily

Lunch
11:00 A.M. until 2:00 P.M.
Daily

Dinner
5:30 P.M. until 10:00 P.M.
Daily

For reservations
(recommended for dinner)
call (912) 924-1555

Jo Childers, who spearheaded the revitalization of downtown Americus, and the descendants of the families who erected the hotel chose to reset this Victorian jewel.

The three-story atrium lobby is Moorish, with handsome arches, wrought-iron railings, hand-carved wooden floral-pattern balusters, and oak floors. An oval banquette with fringe—a Victorian hallmark—commands center stage in the dramatic lobby. A round banquette with floral topiary has the same significance in the magnificent dining room.

For dinner, I enjoyed the Veal Chop Amaretto. Coffee beans in a sauce of amaretto made this dish so juicy that it came in first as the best veal I've ever had. I also tasted the restaurant's Baked Grouper and was surprised at the even-textured, non-"fishy" taste.

Dessert was a special surprise called a Praline Tulip. The Windsor makes a paper-thin praline shell shaped like a tulip and fills it with ice cream, chocolate, and a raspberry sauce. It put the right finishing touch on a superb meal.

After dinner, I visited the perfectly round bridal suite, located at the top of its own set of stairs. It is rumored that when Al Capone stayed here, one of his henchmen was stationed at the bottom of the stairs with a Tommy gun in tow.

The hotel has a ghost that only makes herself known on Sundays in the service elevator. The staff refuses to use the elevator that day.

The Windsor is indeed a fabulous restaurant "with rooms attached"—and, oh, the stories those rooms do tell.

Windsor Hotel's Veal Chop Amaretto

10-ounce, 1¼-inch-thick veal chop
salt and pepper to taste
¼ cup coffee beans, crushed
2 teaspoons butter
1 teaspoon shallots, chopped fine

2 tablespoons amaretto
¼ cup brown sauce
  (favorite recipe)
¼ cup heavy cream

Season veal chop with salt and pepper. Press coffee beans into chop on both sides. Melt butter and sauté chop to medium doneness. Remove chop from pan; reserve and keep warm. Add shallots to pan and sauté until glossy. Deglaze pan with amaretto. Add brown sauce to pan and reduce to half of original volume. Add cream and reduce to half volume. Place chop on warm plate and top with sauce. Serves 1 generously.

Windsor Hotel's Baked Grouper

2 8-ounce grouper fillets
¾ cup lime juice
4 dashes hot sauce
parchment paper
1 medium onion, sliced thin
1 medium green bell pepper,
  julienned

4 stalks celery, julienned
2 medium tomatoes, sliced thin
salt and pepper to taste
thyme

Wash fillets and blot dry. Combine lime juice and hot sauce and marinate grouper for 2 hours. Place fish on large-enough squares of parchment paper to wrap securely. Add onion, bell pepper, and celery around sides of fish; top with tomato slices. Add salt and pepper and sprinkle with thyme. Add remaining marinade. Wrap fillets securely and bake in a preheated 350-degree oven for 15 to 20 minutes, depending on thickness. Serves 2.

Windsor Hotel's Southern Corn Chowder

½ cup butter
1 medium onion, minced
2 stalks celery, minced
2 cloves garlic, minced
1 red bell pepper, minced
1 green bell pepper, minced

1 sprig thyme, minced
1½ pounds corn, cut from the cob
1 cup white wine
salt and pepper to taste
2 quarts heavy cream
½ cup parsley, chopped

Melt butter in a large soup pot or kettle and sauté next 6 ingredients until glossy. Add corn and wine and simmer for 5 minutes. Add salt and pepper and stir in cream; simmer to desired thickness. Sprinkle parsley on top of each bowl. Serves 10.

Dr. Hatchett's Drug Store
Museum and Soda Fountain

On the Square
LUMPKIN

As you walk over the creaking heart-pine floors of this 1892 building, you'll hear fifties bebop music in the background. Owners Andy and Pam Moye know that the period isn't right, but the music seems to fit with walls filled with hair restorers and nerve tonics.

Before you straddle a seat at the soda fountain, know that neither Dr. James Marion Hatchett nor his pharmacist son ever had a drugstore in Lumpkin, much less a soda fountain. According to the "ways of old," the son, Dr. Samuel Callaway Pope Hatchett, ran the drugstore after his father's death in 1894. Samuel's "ways" were to discourage as many customers as he could by his antisocial attitude, which made his marriage at the age of eighty something of a stunner.

The original Hatchett Drug Store was located in Fort Gaines, but its contents were moved to their present location on Lumpkin's square. Today, they reside in this ironwork-trimmed building, which, ironically, once had another drugstore as an occupant.

Take a look at the shelves. They abound with such remedies as Bradford's Female Regulator (which contained 15 to 20 percent alcohol), the Hatchetts' private-label drugs, and other bygone remedies that will send you into gales of laughter. The Moyes have cut a walkway through to the pharmacy in order to display tools used to pulverize and mix doctors' potions.

As overhead paddle fans whirred, I slipped into an aqua leather booth for lunch. Remember those flavored fountain Cokes? You can get a cherry, vanilla, chocolate, or lemon one here, just like you used to buy for a nickel.

Every day, the restaurant's quiche is different, but it's always served with homemade Muffins and a light and tasty Frozen Fruit Salad. My Ham and Spinach Quiche had a richer taste than most quiches. The Chicken Tetrazzini reminded me of my grandmother's recipe, with its plump chicken chunks and perfectly cooked noodles. One of the nicest surprises was Dora's Roast Beef, named for Dora Hudson,

Lunch
11:00 A.M. until 6:00 P.M.
Daily

Dinner
Until 8:00 P.M.
Friday

Reservations
(recommended for groups)
call (912) 838-6924

who does a little of everything at the soda fountain. I also discovered that a specialty of the soda fountain is a spin on a banana split called a South Georgia Split. My hosts said that nobody could finish one!

Dr. Hatchett's is a must for nostalgia buffs and those who like honest-to-goodness old-time food.

Dr. Hatchett's Chicken Tetrazzini

6 ounces dry spaghetti,
 broken in half
1½ cups cooked white chicken meat,
 cut in 1-inch chunks
2 ounces chopped pimientos
dash of Tabasco sauce
2 tablespoons green bell pepper,
 cut in slivers
3 chopped green onions,
 including tops

10¾-ounce can chicken
 mushroom soup
¼ cup chicken broth
2½ tablespoons dry sherry
2 tablespoons heavy cream
6 ounces fresh mushrooms,
 sautéed in butter
salt and pepper to taste
1⅛ cups grated cheddar cheese
3½ tablespoons Parmesan cheese

Cook and drain spaghetti. Combine all ingredients except ⅛ cup of the cheddar and 2 tablespoons of the Parmesan; mix with spaghetti. Place mixture in a 1- to 1½-quart buttered casserole dish and sprinkle with reserved cheeses. Cover and bake in a preheated 350-degree oven for 45 minutes; remove cover during last 10 minutes. Serves 6.

Dr. Hatchett's Frozen Fruit Salad

50 ounces mixed fruit,
 fresh or frozen (defrosted)
8 ounces cream cheese
½ cup powdered sugar
⅓ cup mayonnaise
2 teaspoons vanilla extract

¼ cup burgundy poppy
 seed dressing (commercial)
½ cup chopped pecans
2 cups mini marshmallows
¾ cup whipping cream

Drain fruit. Beat together cream cheese and sugar; blend in mayonnaise. Add vanilla and dressing. Gently fold in fruit, pecans, and marshmallows. Whip cream and fold into mixture. Pour into paper-lined muffins tins. Cover and freeze. Defrost 10 minutes before serving. Serves 24.

Dr. Hatchett's Dora's Roast Beef

5-pound beef rump roast
1 package meat loaf seasoning
1 onion, sliced

1 small green bell pepper,
   seeded and sliced
seasoned salt to taste

Place roast in a crockpot. Add remaining ingredients and cover with water; cook on low heat overnight. Serves 15.

Dr. Hatchett's South Georgia Split

1/3 cup plus 2 tablespoons fresh
   peaches, sliced and sweetened
1 scoop each peach, butter pecan,
   peanut butter, and
   chocolate ice cream
2 tablespoons butterscotch sauce

2 tablespoons chocolate syrup
whipped cream
2 tablespoons roasted peanuts
2 tablespoons pecans
3 whole peanuts, roasted in shell

Distribute 1/3 cup of peaches in a banana split dish. Add the 4 scoops of ice cream, with the peach ice cream toward the middle. Top the butter pecan with the butterscotch sauce, the peanut butter and chocolate with the chocolate syrup, and the peach with reserved peach slices. Top each with a scoop of whipped cream and sprinkle with peanuts and pecans. Top each mound of whipped cream with an in-shell peanut. Serves 1 to 2 generously.

D. Faires

Radium Springs Casino

2501 Radium Springs Road
ALBANY

If you get to Radium Springs early in the morning, you may catch a glimpse of a family of beavers. They come down the Flint River, which flows behind the casino. Blue, glass-clear springs fed by an underground river sparkle just beyond the dining room's windows.

The Creek Indians called the springs "Sky Water" because it looked as if the sky had fallen into the water. Years later, cave drawings, thought to be Creek, were discovered by divers. Many historians believe that it was Radium Springs that Ponce de Leon was searching for in his quest for the Fountain of Youth.

Lunch
10:00 A.M. until 2:00 P.M.
Monday through Saturday

Dinner
5:00 P.M. until 11:00 P.M.
Monday through Saturday

Brunch
11:30 A.M. until 2:00 P.M.
Sunday

For reservations
call (912) 889-0244

A two-story pavilion was built in 1916 for indoor picnicking, dancing, and gambling. But when scientists discovered that the springs contained radium (considered good for your health in the 1920s), the owners reevaluated. Chicago entrepreneur Barron Collier built the handsome Georgian-style Radium Springs Casino in the late 1920s.

Radium Springs attracted both the famous and the infamous. It brought Al Capone, plus droves of people who wanted to swim in the icy water, dance at debutante balls, and gamble. This is where the fortunate played cards, dined, and formed the Indoor Bird Watchers Society, which still exists today. In 1982, the casino was damaged by fire. It was closed until 1990, when a valiant group spent more than $1 million to restore it.

I sat in the lovely cypress dining terrace and enjoyed lunch while watching wildlife through windows that seemed to bring the outdoors inside. The prize for salads has to go to the restaurant's Warm Lamb Salad with Wilted Greens. I also tasted the Fried Green Tomatoes in Tangy Hollandaise Sauce. For dessert, I chose the delicious Crème Caramel.

I was told that the dinner favorites are Pistachio-Crust Salmon in Madeira and Rolled Beef Tenderloin Stuffed with Spinach Mousse. I don't know if I'll come back to swim in the springs' sixty-eight-degree water, but lunch, brunch, or dinner would be a special treat anytime.

Radium Springs Casino's Fried Green Tomatoes in Tangy Hollandaise Sauce

Tangy Hollandaise Sauce

6 egg yolks
¼ teaspoon salt
¼ cup white wine

2 tablespoons white rice vinegar
2 tablespoons lemon juice
1½ cups clarified butter, warm

In the top of a double boiler, beat first 5 ingredients together with a wire whip until eggs are creamy and thick. Remove from heat. Whip butter into egg mixture gradually until consistency is thick.

Tomatoes

2 cups fine cornmeal
1 cup self-rising flour
1 tablespoon salt
1 tablespoon paprika

1½ cups Louisiana Hot Sauce
2 medium green tomatoes,
   sliced ¼-inch thick
1½ cups vegetable oil

Sift first 4 ingredients together in a medium-size bowl. Pour hot sauce into a small bowl. Dip tomato slices in hot sauce, then coat both sides with cornmeal mixture. Heat oil to 350 degrees in a frying pan; fry tomatoes on each side until golden brown. Remove and drain on a paper towel.

Serve with Tangy Hollandaise Sauce. Serves 4.

Radium Springs Casino's Crème Caramel

2 cups sugar
2 tablespoons water
1 tablespoon lemon juice
10 eggs

1 quart milk
2 tablespoons vanilla extract
fresh fruit for garnish

Combine 1 cup sugar, water, and lemon juice in a heavy saucepan over medium heat. Bring to a boil. Stir constantly for 8 minutes until mixture turns a caramel color. *Do not burn*. Pour into individual ovenproof molds (1 tablespoon per mold) or an 8-cup mold. Beat eggs with a wire whip, gradually adding remaining 1 cup sugar, until foamy. Scald milk; add to mixture in a thin, steady stream. Whisk in vanilla. Pour over caramel mixture and set in a hot water bath, allowing water to reach halfway up molds. Bake in a preheated 300-degree oven 1 hour until firm but not brown. Cool and decorate with fresh fruit. Serves 8.

Radium Springs Casino's Warm Lamb Salad with Wilted Greens

Warm Lamb Salad

4 cups lamb, diced	*1 small red onion, diced*
2 tablespoons extra-virgin olive oil	*2 cloves garlic, minced*
1 medium red bell pepper, diced	*1 cup artichoke hearts, diced*
1 medium yellow bell pepper, diced	*salt and pepper to taste*
1 medium green bell pepper, diced	

Sauté lamb in 1 tablespoon olive oil until cooked. Set aside and strain off liquid. Add remaining oil and sauté peppers, onion, garlic, and artichoke hearts until clear. Return lamb to pan and add salt and pepper. Keep warm.

Wilted Greens

1 small bunch turnip greens, cleaned and dried	*2 tablespoons balsamic vinegar* *salt and pepper to taste*

In a hot sauté pan, quickly toss greens with vinegar until they start to wilt. Remove and add salt and pepper.

To serve, place hot greens on plates and top with Warm Lamb Salad. Serves 4 to 6.

Tarrer Inn

On the Square
COLQUITT

At the prestigious Tarrer Inn, calling women "miss" without regard to age or marital status continues to be the respectful way that females are addressed.

The Tarrer Inn looks like a rectangular sculpture of pink sherbet with striped awnings beneath its inviting upper balcony. Sitting on Colquitt's historic downtown square, this 1861 stucco structure was built as a boardinghouse. The house burned within a few years but was later rebuilt by a Confederate soldier. Since that turbulent period, it has housed several different occupants, but it did not achieve fame until Ma Harrell took over as cook at the Hunter House in 1905. When her popularity spread, horse-driven carriages would transport vacationing guests from the train station to Ma Harrell's just for her yeast rolls and fried chicken.

After a $2.5 million renovation, the exquisitely decorated inn has been listed on the National Register of Historic Places. Portraits in the parlor honor Ruth Tarrer Jinks and her husband, the late G. C. Jinks, Sr., who bequeathed money for the restoration.

The inn's three Victorian-appointed dining rooms and twelve individually designed bedrooms look as if they came out of a Laura Ashley scrapbook. What sets this inn apart are its little touches: the parlor tea set, which sits on a tiered table beside an antique burgundy velvet fainting couch; the trompe l'oeil painted bedroom mantels draped with hand-tatted scarves; the tiny ficus-tree centerpieces on each candlelit dining table, set with old-fashioned silver patterns.

Although the beautiful renovation makes the inn sparkle, I discovered that the food is the real star. When I later told my sister that I had Swamp Gravy on my birthday here, she said, "Some people have all the luck." She didn't know that the famous dish, after which Georgia's official folk play is named, is a tribute to the local Mayhaw berry, harvested from the swamps. Swamp Gravy is a bit of a misnomer, as this everything-but-the-kitchen-sink dish is actually a soup.

You've heard of surf and turf, but has it ever been a combination of Rack of Lamb and Salmon in Lobster Davent Sauce? You'll also enjoy the accompanying Zucchini Vegetable Basket and the Twice-Baked Potato. To top off a meal so delicious that you don't want it to end, try the dessert called Blueberry Yogurt Pound Cake. When you visit, you'll understand why I wanted to end neither my dinner nor my stay at this hospitable inn.

Tarrer Inn's Swamp Gravy

8 strips bacon
1 tablespoon fresh basil, chopped fine
¾ teaspoon garlic, minced
¼ cup shallots, chopped
1 cup yellow onions, chopped
½ cup red bell pepper, chopped
½ cup green bell pepper, chopped
¾ cup tomatoes, diced
¼ bunch of broccoli, chopped
¼ head cauliflower, chopped
1 large carrot, sliced diagonally
1 stalk celery, sliced diagonally
½ cup okra, sliced diagonally
¾ cup zucchini, cubed
¾ cup yellow squash, chopped
½ cup red wine
½ tablespoon liquid smoke

½ teaspoon Tabasco sauce
1½ tablespoons Worcestershire sauce
½ gallon beef stock
½ gallon chicken stock
½ gallon fish stock
3½ cups tomato juice
½ pound pork, cooked and chopped bite-size
½ pound beef, cooked and chopped bite-size
½ pound chicken, cooked and chopped bite-size
½ pound fish, cooked and chopped bite-size
1 cup wild rice
salt and pepper to taste

Fry bacon and remove to a paper towel; reserve bacon drippings. Heat drippings in a large stockpot and sauté the next 14 ingredients. Add wine, liquid smoke, Tabasco, Worcestershire, stocks, and tomato juice and stir to combine. Add meats and simmer, stirring periodically, 4 to 6 hours until volume is reduced by ⅓. Cook rice, add to mixture, and cook another hour. Season with salt and pepper. Serves 20.

Tarrer Inn's Twice-Baked Potato

3 2½-inch baking potatoes
2 strips bacon
1 tablespoon butter
¼ to ½ teaspoon minced garlic
pinch of chives, diced fine
¼ teaspoon diced shallots

2 tablespoons sour cream
½ cup heavy whipping cream
salt and pepper to taste
2 tablespoons freshly grated
  Parmesan cheese
paprika to taste

Bake potatoes in a 350-degree oven for 40 to 50 minutes. Fry bacon and drain on a paper towel. Melt butter with bacon drippings and sauté garlic, chives, and shallots until soft. Scoop out potatoes, place in a mixing bowl, and mash with sour cream and whipping cream. Season with salt and pepper and fold in sautéed mixture. Pipe potato mixture back into shells with a pastry tube or spoon potatoes into shells. Sprinkle with Parmesan and paprika. Run potatoes under broiler until cheese begins to melt. Serves 4.

The Grand Old House and Tavern

502 South Broad Street
THOMASVILLE

$\mathcal{T}$oday, we build a new home wherever we want, but you need only turn back the pages of history to discover that this has not always been the case. The country house of prosperous cotton plantation owner Elijah L. Neel was in a prime location for the dreaded malaria. That was near the turn of the century, before modern medicine could successfully treat this life-taking fever. So Neel and his wife, Martha, took the only preventive measure they knew to protect their family. In 1907, they built a magnificent new home in the heart of Thomasville, far from the dread contagion. On my visit to this beautiful house almost entirely encircled by live oaks and palm trees, I was reminded of the party at Twelve Oaks in *Gone With the Wind*.

Lunch
11:30 A.M. until 2:30 P.M.
Wednesday through Saturday

Dinner
6:00 P.M. until 9:30 P.M.
Monday through Saturday

For reservations
(suggested)
call (912) 227-0108

You have your choice, at The Grand Old House, of seven dining rooms, all lovely. Downstairs is the tavern, which is decorated like a traditional English pub, with rafters and brick floors. It caters to a casual crowd with bistro foods—char-grilled steaks and chicken, soups, and salads. Upstairs, my favorite spot is the terrace, with its view of the silver-colored moss draping the oaks.

The menu is revised daily. For lunch, you may choose among, say, Lobster Bisque, Soft-Shell Crab Caesar, Fettuccine and Smoked Salmon, and Chicken Salad with Fresh Fruit. For dinner, how about Pork Tenderloin and Clams Portugaise, Bahamian-Style Lobster Tails, and Grouper Meunière? And for dessert, don't forget Gâteau L'Orange—layers of baked meringue, slivered almonds, and Grand Marnier with Orange Butter Cream in the center and Crème Anglaise on the plate. Hungry yet?

Go right ahead and whip up a batch of that Grouper Meunière if you like—it's really, really good—but for the full effect of the food and atmosphere of The Grand Old House, you'll have to come here. It's a journey I recommend.

The Grand Old House's Pork Tenderloin and Clams Portugaise

2 large pork tenderloins
½ teaspoon salt
½ teaspoon freshly ground
  black pepper
¼ teaspoon cayenne pepper
4 teaspoons paprika
1 cup white vinegar
6 cups dry white wine

½ to 1 cup olive oil
2 large spring onions, chopped fine
6 cloves garlic, chopped fine
3 dozen fresh clams, well washed
3 to 4 sprigs fresh cilantro
white rice
French bread

Cut pork into large cubes and place in a glass mixing bowl. Add salt, pepper, cayenne, paprika, vinegar, and wine. Stir to blend, cover, and refrigerate overnight.

Before cooking, drain pork well, reserving the marinade. Heat olive oil in a large pot over medium heat and sauté onions and garlic until soft. Add pork and sauté about 10 minutes. Add the wine marinade to the simmering pork gradually over a 30-minute period; use more wine if necessary. Stir in clams, bring to a boil, and boil covered for 8 to 10 minutes. Add cilantro, stir, and serve with white rice or French bread. Serves 6 to 8.

Grouper Meunière Grand Old House

1 to 1¼ pounds grouper fillets
salt and pepper to taste
½ cup light vegetable oil
2 eggs
1 cup milk
1 cup flour

¼ cup white wine
¼ cup butter
½ cup fresh parsley, chopped
juice of 1 lemon
1 lemon, peeled and diced
2 teaspoon capers

Wash fillets and pat dry with paper towels. Season with salt and pepper. Heat vegetable oil in a sauté pan until hot. Beat eggs with milk. Dip fillets in flour, then in the egg mixture, then in flour again. Place fillets in the sauté pan. Fry on medium heat for 5 to 7 minutes on each side. Remove fish to a plate. Drain oil from pan and add wine, butter, parsley, and lemon juice, heating to a boil. Add diced lemon and capers, stir well, top fillets with sauce, and serve. Serves 4.

The Grand Old House's Fettucine and Smoked Salmon

10 ounces fettuccine
2 teaspoons butter
¾ cup light cream
3 green onions or chives

4 ounces or more smoked salmon,
cut into bite-size pieces
salt and white pepper to taste

Cook fettuccine in boiling, salted water for 6 to 8 minutes. Drain. Melt butter in a large skillet and add cream and onions. Heat to the boiling point but do not boil. Add salmon and heat for 2 minutes. Pour cooked fettuccine into the skillet with the salmon mixture and stir. Season with salt and pepper. Stir over heat for 2 minutes and serve. Serves 5 to 6.

Susina Plantation Inn

1420 Meridian Road
(12 miles south of Thomasville, Georgia,
22 miles north of Tallahassee, Florida; follow the signs off U.S. 319)

The soft patter of rain through the mossy live oaks, the occasional caw of a blackbird, and the creaking of my old wicker swing were the only sounds that broke the silence on Susina's upstairs porch. It was 1841 when James and Harriet Blackshear built this white-columned Greek Revival mansion, and if I hadn't noticed a telephone pole before winding up the dirt path to the plantation, I wouldn't have known I was in this century.

Another victim of this confusion is the spirit of Mrs. Blackshear, who, it is said, "takes

death as a mere inconvenience" in the routine of overseeing her old home. Widowed with five young children and given the task of producing 235 bales of cotton, Mrs. Blackshear became a rather remarkable figure in her day, winning the respect of her contemporaries. So it is understandable that she didn't want to lose this public esteem after her death. Though her spirit has never actually been seen by succeeding Susina owners, many have heard dogs whining, their hair on end, just before the sound of Mrs. Blackshear's rustling skirt reached their own ears, followed by a breeze sweeping through the room.

Try as I might to evoke her presence by singing old songs I once sang as a child in my grandmother's porch swing, no spirit appeared. What I did notice was the aroma of fresh bread, so I descended the curving staircase. In the mauve-colored living room, guests were having a drink as they swapped quail-hunting tales.

A large antique table for twelve is the focus of the airy dining room, which is decorated in shades of blue and white and features Empire serving pieces. Antique blue-and-white china graces the table. In such an intimate setting, you quickly become acquainted with the guests, and before you know it, you feel as if you've been invited to a grand dinner party. That heavenly bread whose aroma had reached upstairs was everything I imagined it would be. For dinner, I chose the Asparagus Soup and the Crepes with Shrimp—both excellent decisions, as I discovered, and easy to duplicate at home. It is a rare thing to find recipes which are impressive, tasty, and relatively easy to prepare.

Pecan Pie and Apple Pie are good choices for dessert at Susina, as was my delectable Strawberry Shortcake. But the wisest choice of all is electing to experience this romantic page of our past.

Susina Plantation Inn's Crepes with Shrimp

Shrimp filling

¼ stick unsalted butter
¼ medium onion, chopped
¼ teaspoon thyme
dash of cayenne pepper

salt and pepper to taste
1½ cups heavy cream
36 medium shrimp, peeled

Melt butter in a sauté pan and cook onion until soft. Add seasonings and cream and cook for 1 minute. Add shrimp. Cook until shrimp are pink.

Crepes

¾ cup all-purpose flour
½ teaspoon sugar
¼ teaspoon salt

2 eggs
1 cup milk

Sift or stir together flour, sugar, and salt. In another bowl, beat eggs and milk until well blended, then add the flour mixture and stir. Spray a crepe pan or a small frying pan with nonstick coating and heat over a medium flame. Pour ⅙ of the batter in the pan and swirl it around to coat. When the crepe sets, flip it over to brown the other side. Keep crepes warm while preparing the rest; spray the pan with nonstick coating between crepes to prevent sticking.

Just before serving, place a crepe on each of 6 warm plates, fill with 2 tablespoons of shrimp filling, and roll up. Serves 6.

Susina Plantation Inn's Asparagus Soup

½ stick unsalted butter
¼ onion, chopped
1 pound asparagus
2 cups water

2 chicken bouillon cubes
salt and pepper to taste
½ cup heavy cream
2 cups milk

Heat butter in a saucepan and cook onion until soft. Cut off the tough ends of the asparagus; cut the stems into 1-inch pieces and add them to the onions, reserving the tops. Add 1 cup of the water and simmer for 15 minutes. Pour asparagus-onion mixture into a blender and purée. Then pour the purée back into the saucepan, adding remaining 1 cup water, reserved asparagus tips, and bouillon cubes. Cook slowly for 30 minutes. Season with salt and pepper. Add cream and milk, heat briefly, and serve. Serves 6.

Whitfield's

514 Mary Street
WAYCROSS

$\mathcal{W}$hitfield's reminds me of the old song "Hernando's Hideaway." I don't know why it should, because Hernando's Hideaway isn't even a real place, and Whitfield's is not only real but good. Probably, it's the stairs. To get to Whitfield's, you go to downtown Waycross and find a large Charleston limestone building with a staircase running up the side. You can't miss it. At that point, you have a choice: go downstairs to the tavern and through the main floor to the regular dining room, or go up those stairs.

Lunch

11:00 A.M. until 2:00 P.M.
Monday through Saturday

Dinner

6:00 P.M. until 10:00 P.M.
Monday through Thursday

6:00 P.M. until 11:00 P.M.
Friday and Saturday

For reservations
(recommended,
especially on weekends)
call (912) 285-9027

Let's say you're not able to resist an adventure. Climb those stairs, open the door, and there you are. Before you is a large, dark room with a heart-pine floor and wainscoted and papered walls. A fire glints in the fireplace. The room is dotted with white-linen-covered tables and punctuated with enormous fan-topped windows. In one corner is a grill where men in white jackets are carrying in salads and desserts. The restaurant serves a limited menu of steaks and seafood. The cooks at the grill know exactly what the word *rare* means, so if you don't mean it, don't say it. Beyond the grill is the bar, a narrow room where you can sit in quiet or boisterous elegance and sip a preprandial drink.

Do try, when eating here, to glance out the window occasionally. There seem to be more stars visible in Waycross than in other places, and the sight on a clear night is stunning, suggestive of what night must have been like before the advent of cities.

A hundred years ago, people were dancing in this room, looking out at those same stars. In 1907, Whitfield's was the ballroom of Waycross's new Elks Club. For thirty years—through World War I, the Roaring Twenties, and the crash of 1929—people danced and drank here. Then, in 1937, the Elks moved out. Maybelle Carter opened the Carter House Family Buffet downstairs and, for a generation, fed those who could pay and those who could not. At

Whitfield's, the tradition of good times and good food continues. Continuity seems important here, and judging from the quality of the steak I had, this restaurant is onto a good thing.

Whitfield's Almond Amaretto Ice Cream

Almond Crunch Topping

2 ounces sliced almonds   *1 tablespoon water*
1 cup sugar

Spread almonds in a buttered pan. In a small, heavy saucepan, stir together sugar and water over low heat until sugar melts. Pour mixture over almonds and let harden. When the topping is completely cold, break it up with your fingers or a kitchen hammer and grind it in a blender into smaller bits. Store topping in a covered jar in the refrigerator.

½ gallon vanilla ice cream   *8 tablespoons amaretto liqueur*

Freeze parfait or wine glasses. Just before serving, spoon in ice cream, splash with amaretto, and sprinkle with Almond Crunch Topping. Serves 8.

Whitfield's Shrimp with Crabmeat Stuffing

Crabmeat Stuffing

1 stalk celery   *½ teaspoon dill weed*
1 small onion   *¼ teaspoon pepper*
½ bell pepper   *8 ounces crabmeat*
1 stick butter   *½ cup breadcrumbs*
½ cup wine   *1 egg*
¼ teaspoon garlic powder

Chop celery, onion, and bell pepper and sauté in butter. Add wine, garlic powder, dill weed, and pepper, then simmer for 10 minutes. Add crabmeat and breadcrumbs and let mixture sit for 2 minutes. Stir in egg and let stuffing cool.

Shrimp

4 pounds colossal shrimp
  (approximately 10 to a pound)
¾ cup flour

½ teaspoon baking powder
1 egg
¾ cup ice water

Prepare shrimp by shelling and butterflying them; cut them from the underside almost through, to form a pocket. Remove the vein, if necessary, by pulling it out from the underside rather than cutting the top of the shrimp.

Stuff shrimp with Crabmeat Stuffing and lay them on a tray in the freezer for a few minutes until they become manageable. (They may also be prepared ahead and frozen.) Just before serving, combine flour, baking powder, and egg and add water until mixture is the consistency of pancake batter. Dip shrimp in the batter and deep-fry them. Serves 8 as an entrée or 18 as an appetizer.

Note: Leftover stuffing can be used to stuff mushrooms, which also can be battered and fried.

Blueberry Hill

Route 1
HOBOKEN

$\mathcal{G}$oing to Blueberry Hill is a little like going to heaven — occasionally, you are bound to wonder if it is worth the effort. Once you get there, however, all doubts are dispelled. You find such an unusual treat that before you leave you are already planning your second trip. In that respect, of course, it isn't anything like heaven at all.

Blueberry Hill sits in the middle of a pine wood near the

Dinner
5:30 P.M. until 10:00 P.M.
Wednesday through Saturday

On Wednesday, shrimp seconds
are on the house.

For reservations
(recommended)
call (912) 458-2605

Okefenokee Swamp. It's hard to believe that this same building was in service a hundred years ago as a tobacco barn in Pierce County. It was reconstructed on a new site as a mortar-and-log cabin with a cedar-shake roof. Later, it became a seafood restaurant.

Part of its appeal lies in its perfect combination of crab-shack and peat-bog décor. My husband and I first visited during a December rain. The hostess hurried us across the porch, where guests can sit in better weather, and into the main room, where we were escorted to a place before the warm fire.

My husband, whose taste in restaurants runs to French and centrally heated, looked churlish and began to feed the fire. I, the crab-shack connoisseur, was more hopeful. The restaurant had all the requisites on my private list for places that fry mouth-watering shrimp and hush puppies. I was right. But it also does fancier things well. My husband ate his Shrimp Iberville — Blueberry Hill's specialty of shrimp and mushrooms in a sherry sauce, topped with cheddar cheese — and pronounced it delicious. Other entrées include Broiled Sea Bass, Oysters Bienville, and Cajun Stuffed Shrimp. Dessert offerings are definitely in keeping with the name of the restaurant — Hot Blueberry Pie, Cheesecake with Blueberry Sauce, and the Country Bumpkin, a hot blueberry muffin served with ice cream and blueberry topping.

As we bumped our way back to the main road, my husband noted casually that though Blueberry Hill is a long way from home, it is a mere forty miles from the beach where we rent a house every summer. It would be a simple matter to drive over and have dinner a couple of times a week. Wouldn't it?

Blueberry Hill's Shrimp and Eggplant Casserole

1 pound shrimp
1 pound crabmeat
4 slices white bread
4 eggs
6 ounces canned evaporated milk
½ cup water
1 large eggplant
½ lemon

1 stick butter
1 cup chopped celery
1 cup chopped Spanish onion
½ teaspoon cayenne pepper
½ teaspoon black pepper
½ cup chopped green onions
1 cup Captain's Wafer crumbs

Peel and devein shrimp and pick crabmeat. Set aside. Place bread, eggs, milk, and water in a mixing bowl. Mix well and set aside. Peel and chop eggplant and place it in a bowl of water into which the lemon half has been squeezed. In a large skillet, melt butter and sauté celery and Spanish onion until tender. Add the bread-egg mixture, the drained eggplant, cayenne pepper, and black pepper to the skillet. Cook and stir until eggplant is tender. Add green onions, shrimp, and crab and cook until shrimp turn pink. Place in a casserole, top with cracker crumbs, and serve. Serves 6.

Note: This dish can be made ahead. Add the crumbs just before serving and reheat briefly in a microwave.

Blueberry Hill's Shrimp Chablisienne

1 stick butter
1 cup diced green onions
4 tablespoons minced shallots
2 pounds shrimp,
 peeled and deveined

1 cup Chablis
3 ounces cognac
1 teaspoon salt (optional)
½ teaspoon pepper
2 ounces sliced almonds

Melt butter in a frying pan and sauté onions and shallots until wilted. Add shrimp, Chablis, cognac, salt, and pepper and simmer until shrimp are opaque. Sprinkle with almonds and serve in individual ramekins. Serves 4.

Blueberry Hill's Hush Puppies

1 cup self-rising cornmeal
½ cup self-rising flour
1 teaspoon baking powder
dash of salt

1 large onion, grated
1 egg
½ cup milk

Mix all dry ingredients together, then add onion and egg. Add milk, stirring, until batter is the consistency of honey. Drop it by the tablespoonful into a deep fryer heated to 300 degrees and cook until golden brown. Serves 4.

Seagle's

105 Osborne Street
ST. MARYS

There is something about Seagle's in the Riverview Hotel that draws people back. Just what that something is seems hard to define. Built in 1916, it looks like a scene out of a Tennessee Williams play. If you look closely, you can find the watermarks from hurricanes—particularly 1964's Dora—but the lobby with its original Mission Oak furniture has weathered the elements well. At the register, you'll see a cat near a Tiffany lamp, and if you look down to read Roy Crane's yellowed 1930s

Breakfast
7:00 A.M. until 11:00 A.M.
Saturday and Sunday

Dinner
5:00 P.M. until 10:00 P.M.
Monday through Saturday

5:00 P.M. until 9:00 P.M.
Sunday

Reservations are discouraged, but the telephone number is (912) 882-3242.

comic strip featuring the hotel, you'll see the same desk registry and Tiffany lamp, presided over by one of this cat's predecessors. I couldn't believe it either.

Its location on the waterfront has made the hotel easily accessible to shrimpers and other sea people who like to put in for good food in a nostalgic atmosphere. Back in the 1930s when cartoonist Roy Crane came here, he intended to stay a few days but somehow stayed for months. That's the way the Riverview is—you arrive expecting it to be just a stopover and discover how easy it is to lengthen your stay. Crane was so enamored with the Riverview that he frequently drew it in his cartoon strip. I particularly like his description of breakfast at the hotel. A member of the staff tells a newly arrived guest that the hotel serves only a light breakfast: "Jist grits an' hominy an' all the ham an' eggs an' flapjacks you can eat."

Breakfast, I'm told, is a little different from the way it was during Crane's days here. But at dinner, the size of the platters coming out of the kitchen makes it difficult to believe that much has changed in this homey dining room, with its old-fashioned print wallpaper and green draperies. When you are this close to fresh deepwater Rock Shrimp, that is the item to order; the lightly fried shrimp were delightfully succulent. My platter also included some White Shrimp, which I learned were so tasty because they were precooked by the Gulf Stream. You'll also appreciate the homemade Hush Puppies and

French Fries, which I wager taste much as they did years ago. It's little things like these that continue to attract and keep people here.

If you can manage to squeeze in dessert (and you should try), you will enjoy the homemade Rum Chiffon Pie. A smoother pie you won't find. But perhaps you'd prefer the homemade Peanut Butter Pie. Either is definitely worth saving room for.

Seagle's Cashew Shrimp

1 cup chicken broth,
  canned or homemade
¼ pound clam strips
1 tablespoon cornstarch
white pepper to taste
2 eggs
1 tablespoon water

1 cup all-purpose flour
1 pound rock or white shrimp,
  shelled and cleaned
oil for deep-frying
½ pound rice, cooked
4 scallions, chopped
¹/₃ cup cashews, chopped

In a small saucepan, simmer chicken broth with clam strips, stirring frequently. Add cornstarch and white pepper and stir until smooth and slightly thickened; keep warm, stirring occasionally. In a small mixing bowl, mix eggs with water. Place flour in another small bowl. Dip shrimp in egg wash, coat with flour, drop in hot oil, and cook until golden brown. Remove shrimp and drain on a paper towel. Make a bed of rice on 4 plates and spoon equal amounts of shrimp onto each. Cover shrimp with clam sauce and sprinkle with scallions and cashews. Serves 4.

Scallops Seagle's

2 to 3 tablespoons butter
4 scallions, chopped
½ cup fresh mushrooms, sliced

½ cup white wine
1 pound calico or fresh bay scallops
4 slices Swiss cheese

Melt butter in a skillet and sauté scallions and mushrooms until just tender. In a saucepan over simmering heat, combine wine and scallops, making sure each scallop is immersed in wine. Simmer 3 to 5 minutes until scallops are white. Drain. Place scallops on each of 4 plates and ladle with onions and mushrooms. Lay 1 slice of cheese over top of scallops and place under broiler for 1 minute until cheese melts. Serves 4.

Seagle's Rum Chiffon Pie

2 envelopes unflavored gelatin
1 cup cold water
½ cup dark rum
6 egg yolks
¾ cup sugar

1¾ cups whipping cream
1 teaspoon vanilla
2 graham cracker pie shells
grated chocolate for garnish

Soften gelatin in 1 cup cold water. Place in small saucepan over low heat and bring almost to a boil, stirring to dissolve. Let cool. Add rum, stirring until well mixed, then set aside. In a large bowl, beat egg yolks and sugar until very fluffy. Beat gelatin mixture into egg mixture; cool in refrigerator, stirring occasionally, until almost set. In a separate bowl, whip cream with vanilla until it stands in soft peaks, then fold it into gelatin mixture. Pour into pie shells and garnish with chocolate. Chill until set. Yields 2 pies.

Jekyll Island Club

371 Riverview Drive
JEKYLL ISLAND

*E*vidence shows that after feasting on Jekyll Island's fresh oysters, Guale Indians tossed their shells into a huge pile, called a midden. The Guales were drawn to the island for its warm winter climate, hunting, and abundant shellfish. Eight thousand years later, some of America's wealthiest families chose to buy this private island and form a club for the same reasons that had drawn the Guales.

John Eugene duBignon, whose family had owned Jekyll from 1790 to 1860, repurchased the island after the Civil War. He became partners with his brother-in-law, Newton Finney, who moved in New York's elite circles. By 1886, the entrepreneurial Finney persuaded fellow million-aires to buy Jekyll Island and turn it into a private, members-only family resort for hunting and fishing.

Breakfast
7:00 A.M. until 10:00 A.M.
Monday through Saturday

Lunch
11:00 A.M. until 2:00 P.M.
Monday through Saturday

Dinner
6:00 P.M. until 10:00 P.M.
Daily

Brunch
10:45 A.M. until 2:00 P.M.
Sunday

For reservations
(suggested)
call (912) 635-2600

A select group of fifty-three captains of industry built the Jekyll Island Club. The asymmetrical Queen Anne design includes sprawling wraparound verandas and a signature turret. By the 1900s, the club was so successful that it was said that the owners of one-sixth of the world's wealth sailed their yachts here for winters of hunting and deal-making. Many business deals that took place here are legend, but none affected the public more than the creation of what later became the Federal Reserve Bank, which occurred secretly in November 1910.

Today, the club has gone through a $20 million renovation in order to provide modern amenities while preserving such things as the croquet lawn, the bike riding, the fishing, and the same opportunities to get close to nature that were available in yesteryear.

As always, a comfortable elegance prevails. The Grand Dining Room was designed to dazzle, and it still does. A double row of Ionic columns cuts through the center to the room's focal point—a handsome fireplace. I sat near the fireplace and was welcomed with the club's version of champagne, a twist on the famous Kir Royale. And you know you're in Georgia when you taste the fresh Georgia White Shrimp, served with Brandy Cream Sauce. I was especially impressed with the Baked Vidalia Onion Salad, which looked like a big white rose and had a delicate, subtle taste.

The "continental American" entrées have a slight low country leaning. The Lamb Chops en Croute are a rich-bodied concoction. Another excellent choice is the Veal Pork Sausage Mousseline.

The dessert tray is a wicked device because it's too tempting to refuse. A friend of mine, advising me about the Macadamia Nut Torte, said, "I should never have taken the first bite." Naturally, I had to try this pitfall of chocolate, nuts, and whipped cream, and I hope that when you visit this former millionaires' paradise, you will, too.

Jekyll Island Club's Lamb Chops en Croute

4 large lamb chops, Frenched	4 links sausage
salt and white pepper to taste	1 egg white
1½ ounces lamb scraps	¼ teaspoon sage
1½ ounces veal round	1 sheet pastry dough
1½ ounces pork loin	1 egg yolk
1 strip bacon	1 teaspoon water

Sear lamb chops in a pan. Add salt and pepper, remove, and reserve in warm oven. Purée lamb scraps, veal, pork loin, bacon, and sausage in a food processor. Fold in egg white and sage. Spread mousseline on both sides of reserved lamb chops and wrap in rolled-out pastry dough. Whisk egg yolk with water and brush top and seams of pastry. Bake at 425 degrees about 25 minutes until golden brown.

Lamb Jus

1 pound lamb bones	1 or 2 bouillon cubes
3 cups water	1 bay leaf
salt and pepper to taste	1 sprig fresh rosemary
1 clove garlic, chopped	

Brown lamb bones and add water, salt and pepper, garlic, bouillon, and bay leaf. Bring to a boil, lower heat to medium, and reduce by half. Add rosemary and simmer for 45 minutes. Strain.

To serve, place cooked Lamb Chops en Croute on warmed dishes and ladle Lamb Jus over top. Serves 4.

Jekyll Island Club's Baked Vidalia Onion Salad

4 Vidalia onions, with skin
2 strips bacon, diced
2 ounces onion, diced
1 tablespoon butter
1 cup apple juice
2 tablespoons orange marmalade

¼ teaspoon basil
¼ teaspoon oregano
½ teaspoon cornstarch
1 tablespoon sugar
salt and pepper to taste
lettuce

Bake Vidalia onions for 1 hour at 400 degrees. Let cool and set aside. Sweat bacon and 2 ounces onion in butter until barely tender. Add apple juice, marmalade, basil, and oregano. Bring to a boil and stir in cornstarch. Add sugar and salt and pepper. Peel outer skin of Vidalia onions and cut in small sections. Peel back onion segments into flower petals. Top with dressing and place on lettuce. Serves 4.

The King and Prince Beach and Golf Resort

ST. SIMONS ISLAND

$\mathcal{S}$itting down for lunch, I looked through palm trees to see the ocean gently breaking upon the beach. Even on a cloudy day, that view is like having a backrub—tension just seems to ease with the flow of the tide. The view is just one reason for the feeling of tranquility at this resort.

When you first enter the hotel, the atrium features a heated pool and a Jacuzzi surrounded by large, lush plants; you know immediately that this is a hotel devoted to leisure living. Another appealing feature is the old ballroom converted into a dining room. The stained-glass lunettes above the French doors provide diners with a pictorial history of the island.

My surroundings lent import to my luncheon choices. Sitting in the Tavern Restaurant, which overlooks the ocean, I naturally thought of seafood, of which the Seafood Gumbo is a stellar example. My companion pronounced the Crabmeat Quiche worthy of Neptune himself. We enjoyed a bite of the honey-flavored Muffins and quickly understood why guests take a few along for the road.

The next morning, I enjoyed the buffet breakfast in the Delegal Room, named for Lieutenant Delegal, who built the first fort on St. Simons in 1736. Fearing Spanish invasion, the cunning Delegal dressed all the islanders in British uniforms, lined them single file across the beaches flanking his fort, then fired his cannons so rapidly that the Spaniards retreated from this illusion of massive troops.

Although the forts are gone, this 1935 hotel still proudly boasts Spanish Colonial architecture and an elegant English Colonial interior. It is no wonder that it has retained its distinction as a "Kingdom by the Sea."

Tavern Restaurant—
Breakfast
7:00 A.M. until 10:30 A.M.
Daily

Lunch
11:00 A.M. until 2:00 P.M.
Daily

Dinner
2:00 P.M. until 10:00 P.M.
Daily

Delegal Room—
Buffet Breakfast
7:00 A.M. until 10:30 A.M.
Daily

For reservations
call (912) 638-3631

The King and Prince's Muffins

1¼ cups rolled oats
1 cup buttermilk
1 egg
¾ cup brown sugar
½ stick butter or margarine,
  melted and cooled
¾ cup flour

1 teaspoon baking powder
½ teaspoon salt
½ teaspoon baking soda
½ cup raisins
½ cup pecans
honey
butter

Combine oats and buttermilk in a mixer bowl and let stand for 1 hour. Add egg, sugar, and melted butter. Mix for 30 seconds with an electric mixer; scrape down the bowl. Add dry ingredients, raisins, and pecans. Mix on low speed about 15 seconds until moist. Grease muffin tins or use cupcake liners and fill half full. Bake at 350 degrees for 15 minutes. Serve with honey and butter. Makes 1 dozen muffins.

The King and Prince's Seafood Gumbo

2 tablespoons bacon fat
3 tablespoons flour
8-ounce package frozen okra
  or 1 cup sliced fresh okra
2 tablespoons margarine
1 cup chopped Spanish onions
1 cup chopped celery
½ cup chopped and
  seeded green peppers
¼ cup chopped fresh parsley
½ teaspoon chopped garlic
6 cups chicken stock

10-ounce can chopped tomatoes
2 tablespoons Worcestershire sauce
1 bay leaf
⅛ teaspoon cayenne pepper
½ teaspoon Tabasco sauce
½ teaspoon ground cumin
½ teaspoon thyme
½ cup white wine
¾ pound medium shrimp
½ pound sea scallops
2 cups cooked rice

Heat bacon fat in a cast-iron pot and gradually add flour, stirring and cooking slowly for 45 minutes until roux is a dark chocolate color. In a separate pan, sauté okra in margarine for 15 minutes. Add to the roux. Add remaining ingredients except shrimp, scallops, and rice and simmer for 2 hours. Just before serving, add shrimp and scallops and cook 5 to 10 minutes until shrimp are pink and scallops are cooked through. To serve, put 3 to 4 tablespoons rice in each of 6 soup bowls and add gumbo. Serves 6.

The King and Prince's Crabmeat Quiche

9-inch deep-dish pie shell

½ cup chopped Spanish onions

½ cup chopped celery

½ cup sliced mushrooms

½ cup chopped artichoke hearts

2 tablespoons butter or margarine

8 ounces frozen crabmeat, thawed

¾ cup shredded cheddar cheese

¾ cup Monterey Jack cheese

5 eggs

1 cup milk

¾ cup half-and-half

½ teaspoon ground nutmeg

½ teaspoon garlic powder

1 teaspoon salt

1 teaspoon ground black pepper

Prick piecrust and place it in a 350-degree oven for 5 to 7 minutes until lightly browned. In a nonstick sauté pan, cook onions, celery, mushrooms, and artichokes in butter until soft. Drain crabmeat, pick out any bits of shell, add to sautéed vegetables, and heat through. Combine crab mixture and cheeses in alternating layers in the piecrust, starting and ending with cheeses. Whip together eggs, milk, half-and-half, and remaining ingredients and slowly pour over quiche; fill to the rim but do not let overflow. Place on a baking sheet and bake 30 minutes in a 350-degree oven until set in the center. Let cool for 15 minutes until firm. Serves 5 or more.

The Cloister

SEA ISLAND

$\mathcal{W}$hen was the last time that gingersnaps and milk were waiting for you before bedtime? How long has it been since you had the opportunity to ride a horse along the beach at sunset? And when did you last find yourself in a breathtakingly beautiful setting, with your every need catered to? These are but a few of the amenities that you can expect to find at Sea Island's fabulous resort, The Cloister.

Howard Coffin built this "friendly little hotel" with the help of his cousin Alfred William Jones in 1928. It was never, even in the planning stages, considered to be just another hotel. Coffin hired famed designer Addison Mizner and insisted that The Cloister embody a lifestyle that would make it known as a "place of peace and play and freedom." As you play golf, walk beneath an avenue of majestic oaks dressed with wisps of Spanish moss, or sample the abundance of delectable food, you know that Coffin's dream is a success.

To spend a vacation here is to enjoy the best of good, old-fashioned pampering. It is possible, however, merely to eat here. I do it all the time, forcing my family to take some good clothes to the beach every summer for that purpose. The Cloister has something for everyone—finger bowls and afternoon tea, ice cream cones, and good, stiff Scotch. And the food is great.

The Filet du Boeuf Florentine is a favorite of my husband's. Spinach stuffed into a steak is his idea of the right way to eat vegetables. Now that I have the recipe, it's becoming a special-occasion staple at our house. And the thing that I like best about the menu is its attention to would-be skinny people like me, who don't want to sit in a nice dining room and gnaw miserably on a few steamed broccoli spears. The Cloister has for years offered light cuisine that actually

Breakfast
Main Dining Room
7:00 A.M. until 9:30 A.M.
Daily

Beach Club
7:00 A.M. until 10:30 A.M.
Daily

Lunch
Noon until 2:00 P.M.
Daily

Dinner
7:00 P.M. until 9:00 P.M.
Daily

For reservations
(required)
call (912) 638-3611

tastes good. A person can eat well here and not waddle away from the table. Try the Chocolate Mousse if you don't believe me—it's the perfect light dessert.

After dinner, you can dance in the clubrooms or do what I do—wander around Sea Island and gawk at the houses. You may never live here, but you can take away some swell memories.

The Cloister's Filet du Boeuf Florentine

2 pounds fresh spinach
1 tablespoon butter
½ cup fresh basil, chopped
½ cup Parmesan cheese
3 egg yolks

2 tablespoons garlic, minced
2 tablespoons shallots, minced
5-pound beef tenderloin
salt and pepper

Sauté spinach in butter for 3 or 4 minutes; drain well. In a bowl, mix spinach, basil, Parmesan, egg yolks, garlic, and shallots. Create a pocket by inserting a knife from both ends of the tenderloin until the hole goes all the way through; use a large fork to enlarge the pocket. Stuff the pocket with the spinach mixture until filled. Season outside of tenderloin with salt and pepper and sear it in a hot pan sprayed with a nonstick spray until browned. Place tenderloin in a roasting pan and bake at 350 degrees until an internal temperature of 115 degrees is reached. Let cool for 10 or 15 minutes. Slice and serve. Serves 10.

The Cloister's Chocolate Mousse

6 ⅜ ounces dark chocolate
3 eggs, separated
2 tablespoons plus ¾ teaspoon
    powdered sugar

12 ounces whipped topping
½ cup milk
1½ teaspoons granulated sugar

Melt chocolate in a double boiler. In a large mixing bowl, beat egg yolks and powdered sugar at high speed until a thick ribbon is achieved. Combine whipped topping and milk, mixing a little of the topping with the milk first, and whip on medium speed until desired consistency. Fold ⅓ of the whipped topping into the yolk mixture. Fold in the melted chocolate, then fold in the remaining whipped topping. In a clean bowl, beat the egg whites and granulated sugar to a medium peak. Gently fold egg-white mixture into yolk mixture. Spoon into glasses or fill bowls and smooth the tops. Serves 10.

Note: Four to eight ounces of your choice of liquor may be added as the whipped topping is folded into the yolk mixture. Rum is especially good.

The Cloister's Almond Macaroons

8 ounces almond paste   *2 egg whites*
1 cup granulated sugar   *2 teaspoons sugar*

Process almond paste and 1 cup sugar in a food processor for 1 minute until blended. Add egg whites and process until moist. Drop dough by spoonfuls about 1½ inches apart on greased cookie sheets. Sprinkle with 2 teaspoons sugar. Bake at 350 degrees about 15 minutes until light brown. Slide a spatula under macaroons to loosen while still warm; allow to cool before handling. Yields 30 to 40 macaroons.

Elizabeth on 37th

105 East 37th Street
SAVANNAH

If I lived in Savannah, I'm afraid I'd take its charm for granted. I'd lose that special warmth I felt when I looked through the lens of my camera and saw Spanish moss delicately framing the roof and misting across the upstairs window of Elizabeth on 37th.

Dinner
6:00 P.M. until 10:30 P.M.
Monday through Saturday

For reservations
call (912) 236-5547

Inside this old, elaborate 1900 mansion, copied from a home the Gibbes family saw in Boston, you'll find an enormous fireplace in the spacious foyer. There is another, smaller white-enameled fireplace in the dining room, where I sat within what are known as the "nooks and crannies" of such old homes. When the paint was stripped from these walls, it was discovered that they had once been painted red and washed with silver. That was during the time when the Sprague family, who worked with the Savannah Sugar Refinery and bought the house just before World War II, had made the home a centerpiece for elegant parties.

Since black-eyed peas are almost synonymous with the South, I had to order the Black-Eyed Pea Soup for my appetizer. It is a spicy soup so thick that Northerners might call it a chowder. The flavor of black-eyed peas is there, but that distinct taste combines with roasted quail, fresh red pepper, wild rice, and onions to form one of the heartiest soups imaginable. It is perfect with a glass of Bordeaux. A great wintertime recipe!

For my entrée, I chose the Oyster and Sausage Turnover, which is a terrific, hearty combination of fresh oysters and sausage tempered with three different cheeses. My Asparagus Salad, accented with bacon and pine nuts and served with a lovely, light sauce, was an ideal complement to the turnover.

Since host Michael Terry and chef and owner Elizabeth Terry also bill the restaurant as a dessert cafe, I wasn't about to pass. I set out to try a bit of the Savannah Cream Cake and the Light Chess Pie with Chocolate and Raspberries but ended up eating a lot of both. The cake, featuring cream laced with sherry and a strawberry-raspberry purée, was deliciously smooth, and the pie, a bit richer with its touch of chocolate, was superb.

Elizabeth on 37th's Black-Eyed Pea Soup

16-ounce package
  dried black-eyed peas
8 cups chicken broth
3 ham hocks
2 cups onion, minced
1 cup celery, minced
3 cloves garlic, minced

1 cup dry sherry
1 cup wild rice, cooked
½ cup fresh red peppers
  (or ¼ cup dried)
1 cup smoked chicken, quail,
  or sausage, drained and diced
black pepper to taste

In a large Dutch oven, cover peas with water and let soak overnight. Drain if needed. Add broth and ham hocks and cook, covered, for 1 hour, skimming when necessary. Add onions, celery, and garlic and simmer 30 minutes longer. Remove ham hocks, cut meat from the bones, and return meat to soup with sherry, rice, red pepper, and smoked meat. Season lightly with black pepper. Serves 8 to 10.

Elizabeth on 37th's Light Chess Pie with Chocolate and Raspberries

3 extra-large eggs
1 cup sugar
⅓ cup sour cream
¼ cup cake flour
8-inch piecrust, baked
1 tablespoon butter

1 teaspoon rum
¼ cup semisweet chocolate chips
½ pint fresh raspberries
½ pint heavy whipping cream
1 tablespoon Grand Marnier
  or crème de cassis

Separate eggs and beat whites until stiff but not dry. In another bowl, beat yolks about 4 minutes until pale yellow. Add sugar and mix well, then add sour cream and cake flour until well blended. Gently fold in egg whites. Fill pie shell with mixture and bake at 325 degrees for 10 minutes until custard is set and light brown. Cool. In a small saucepan, make a glaze by melting butter and rum until blended. Remove from heat. Add chocolate. *Do not cook* the chocolate; the hot butter-rum mixture will melt it. Stir and cool. Spread a thin layer of chocolate on the cooled pie. Cover pie with raspberries. Whip cream with Grand Marnier or crème de cassis and pipe or spoon over top of pie in desired design. Yields 1 pie.

Elizabeth on 37th's Oyster and Sausage Turnover

1 pound spicy bulk sausage
1 pint fresh oysters
½ cup raw milk cheddar cheese
  or mild cheddar, grated

¼ cup cream cheese
¼ cup Assiago cheese, grated
8-inch piecrust (favorite recipe)

Sauté sausage and drain on a paper towel. Place oysters under the broiler for 1 minute to firm. Combine sausage, oysters, and cheeses and drain mixture in a sieve. Prepare piecrust dough. Divide dough into quarters and roll out each quarter into a circle. Place 2 or more rounded spoonfuls of sausage mixture on half of each circle, then fold other half over mixture to form a half-moon shape, sealing edges with a fork. Continue until sausage mixture is used up. Bake at 400 degrees for 10 minutes. Serves 4.

The Olde Pink House

23 Abercorn Street
SAVANNAH

*O*ffset in a square of emerald-colored trees, The Olde Pink House glows like a rare jewel. Built in the Georgian style by James Habersham, Jr., in 1771, Savannah's oldest mansion has taken on a pink tinge from its red bricks; through time, the color has seeped through the white stucco. The mansion has housed many se-

crets, none more important than those discussed at the private meetings held by Habersham during the Revolutionary War. After the war, Habersham was a speaker at the state legislature and a trustee of the University of Georgia.

It should be no surprise, then, that such an active man continues to make his presence known. The chandelier was not twirling when I visited the downstairs Tavern Room for a glass of famous Planters Punch, so I assumed that the spirit of James Habersham was content upstairs. Though the ghost has never been seen, everyone knows who lights the candles, rearranges the furniture, and twirls the chandelier — all familiar occurrences.

Each dining room has a mellow richness that transports you back to a refined era. I favor the soft Gold Room, with its handsome eighteenth-century portraits and lovely fireplace. Dining by candlelight from hand-painted china in such a room gives one an intimate glimpse into the past. I savored the herbal taste of the Black Bean Soup and was delighted with the perfect blend of cumin and vegetables in the Riverfront Gumbo. The little accents — such as the Salad served with a tart, creamy dressing, arriving with an ice-cold fork — create this restaurant's unforgettable personality.

The fluffy Yeast Rolls are so deceptively light that you are apt to tuck more than one away. For dinner, I was tempted by the Grilled Pork Tenderloin Crusted with Almonds and Molasses but chose the delicious Black Grouper Stuffed with Blue Crab, served with Vidalia Onion Sauce. The desserts, like the restaurant itself, are without parallel. The rich Sherry Trifle, crunchy Peanut Butter Pie, and smooth Chocolate de Cocoa Almond Pie are edible fantasies.

The Olde Pink House's Sherry Trifle

1½ quarts milk
1½ cups sugar
2 tablespoons cornstarch
6 eggs

½ cup sherry
2 cups cream
1½-pound pound cake, sliced
raspberry or strawberry preserves

Pour milk into the top of a double boiler over hot (not boiling) water. In a mixing bowl, beat together sugar, cornstarch, and eggs until smooth. Add to milk and heat slowly, stirring constantly, until the mixture thickens. Set aside to cool. Add sherry to the cooled custard. In another bowl, whip the cream and set aside. Arrange cake slices in a 13-by-9¼-by-2-inch baking pan. Spread with preserves, then top with a layer of custard and a layer of whipped cream. Repeat until all ingredients are used. Chill. Serves 6 to 8.

The Olde Pink House's Riverfront Gumbo

1 pound meaty ham bone
1 chicken or turkey carcass
   with some meat intact
1 pound beef marrow bones
16-ounce can tomatoes, chopped
3 stalks celery, chopped
2 medium onions, chopped
1 large green pepper, chopped
1 teaspoon or more cumin

1 teaspoon salt
¼ teaspoon freshly ground
   black pepper
1 cup beef stock
1 tablespoon butter
2½ cups sliced okra
17-ounce can whole-kernel corn
½ cup dry red wine
chopped parsley

Place ham bone, chicken carcass, and beef marrow in a large, heavy saucepan. Add tomatoes, celery, onions, green pepper, and seasonings. Cover with water and bring to a boil; reduce heat, cover, and simmer for 2 hours, stirring occasionally to prevent sticking. Remove the bones, leaving the meat. Add beef stock. Stir in butter, okra, corn, and wine. Simmer 30 to 40 minutes. Taste and adjust seasonings. Garnish with parsley before serving. Serves 8.

The Olde Pink House's She-Crab Soup

1½ cups onion, chopped
1½ cups celery, chopped
½ cup red bell pepper, chopped
1 tablespoon fresh thyme, chopped
1 cup butter

3 ounces crab roe
¾ cup plain flour
3 quarts milk
1 pound blue or white crabmeat
salt and pepper to taste

In a large, heavy saucepan, sauté onion, celery, pepper, and thyme in butter. Add crab roe. Stir in flour. Add milk, stirring with a wire whisk. Bring mixture to 200 degrees, stirring often. Add crabmeat. Season with salt and pepper and serve. Serves 6 to 8.

Mrs. Wilkes' Boarding House

107 West Jones Street
SAVANNAH

eople don't help one another as they once did because they are afraid of becoming involved. If that had been Mrs. Wilkes's decision fifty-odd years ago, I wouldn't have been fortunate enough to sit down to what a guest described as one of her "belly-busting good" meals. When an elderly friend who owned a boardinghouse on Jones Street became ill and asked Sema Wilkes to help out, it seemed to Mrs. Wilkes the natural thing to do, since she had always enjoyed cooking for family and friends. So she got involved, an involvement that has brought her down-home cooking to the attention of *David Brinkley's Journal*, the *Today* show, and myself. I first heard about the restaurant up in the Georgia mountains.

Breakfast
8:00 A.M. until 9:00 A.M.
Monday through Friday

Lunch
11:30 A.M. until 3:00 P.M.
Monday through Friday

Reservations are not accepted.
For more information
call (912) 232-5997

Although there was no sign out front to mark the entrance to this 1870 red-brick, three-story "paired house," I could tell it was the place by the long line waiting on the sidewalk. The restaurant is on the ground floor of the house, which still looks very much like an old, respectable boardinghouse. At first, Mrs. Wilkes fed only the boarders, but as news of her cooking spread, she allowed a few friends and neighbors to stop by for dinner. Though it is no longer a boardinghouse, neighbors and friends continue to come, and tourists are made to feel so much at home that they leave as friends.

I sat beside Mrs. Wilkes at a large oak table garnished with her homegrown roses and partook of the parade of bowls. Naturally, I helped myself to a piece of her authentic Fried Chicken and refrained from another piece only because I wanted a taste from each bowl: Creole Eggplant, Pickled Beets, Green Beans, Spaghetti, Sweet Potato Soufflé, Black-Eyed Peas, English Peas and Noodles, Collard Greens, Mashed Potatoes, Squash Casserole, Curried Cabbage, Cornbread Dressing, Macaroni and Cheese, and, of course, lots of hot Biscuits. After a taste of the Boston Cream, Coconut Cream, and Sweet Potato Pies, I understood why this lady hasn't received a complaint in over two million meals, for each dish vies with the next in exceptional good flavor.

The week after my visit, Mrs. Wilkes and her daughter, Margie Martin, were scheduled to cook at Kasteel Belvedere in Brussels as America's representatives of Southern cooking. She told me there was no sign about this out front because it would detract from the home-like atmosphere. It's just this kind of attitude that can take you from a boardinghouse to a castle, when you're willing to get involved.

Mrs. Wilkes' Boarding House's Creole Eggplant

4 tablespoons bacon drippings
3 medium eggplants,
* peeled and cubed*
1 teaspoon salt
½ cup green bell pepper, chopped

½ cup onion, chopped
20-ounce can tomatoes
½ cup ketchup
1 cup corn flakes
Parmesan cheese

In a large Dutch oven, heat 2 tablespoons bacon drippings and sauté eggplant with salt for 5 minutes. In a separate skillet, heat remaining 2 tablespoons bacon drippings and sauté pepper and onion; add to eggplant. Add tomatoes, ketchup, and corn flakes and cook until flavors blend. Pour into a greased baking dish and sprinkle with Parmesan. Bake in a 350-degree oven for 30 minutes. Serves 8.

Mrs. Wilkes' Boarding House's Skillet Squash Au Gratin

¼ cup butter or margarine
4 cups summer squash, sliced thin
1 medium onion, sliced
1 teaspoon salt

dash of pepper
¼ cup water
½ cup cheddar cheese, grated

Melt butter in a saucepan. Add squash, onion, salt, pepper, and water. Cover and cook 10 to 15 minutes until tender. Sprinkle with cheese and serve. Serves 6 to 8.

Mrs. Wilkes' Boarding House's English Peas and Noodles

Cream Sauce

4 tablespoons butter
4 tablespoons all-purpose flour
½ pint cream or milk

4 tablespoons sherry (optional)
salt and pepper to taste

In a saucepan, melt butter and add flour to make a roux. Add cream and stir until smooth and thickened. Stir in sherry and add salt and pepper.

10-ounce package frozen
  English peas
1 tablespoon bacon drippings
1 small onion, minced

1 ham hock
¼ cup mushrooms, chopped
¼ cup noodles, cooked

In a medium saucepan, cook peas with bacon drippings until almost tender. Add onion, ham hock, mushrooms, and noodles.

When ingredients are warm, add ½ cup Cream Sauce and simmer until heated through. Serves 6.

Mrs. Wilkes' Boarding House's Curried Cabbage

2 tablespoons butter or
  bacon drippings
6 cups shredded cabbage
1 teaspoon curry

1 tablespoon salt
salt and pepper to taste
1 cup chopped tomatoes (optional)

In a large skillet, melt butter and add cabbage, curry, and 1 tablespoon salt. Stir, cover, and cook over medium heat for 5 minutes. Add salt and pepper and tomatoes just before cabbage is done. Serves 4 to 5.

45 South at the Pirates' House

20 East Broad Street
SAVANNAH

$\mathcal{W}$hen you dine at a restaurant as upscale as 45 South in the circa 1734 Pirates' House, you overflow with pleasant adjectives. Five of the Pirates' House's twenty-three dining rooms have undergone a transformation that has turned them into the tony 45 South. Although 45 South is only an interior door away from the Pirates' House, the atmosphere is miles removed. At the Pirates' House, guests enjoy a fun, family-oriented restaurant with framed pages of Robert Louis Stevenson's *Treasure Island* on the walls of the Captain's Room. Some of the real-life events fictionalized in the book supposedly took place here. Reportedly, short-handed captains drugged visiting sailors, robbed them, and carried them unconscious through a block-long tunnel to waiting ships in Savannah's harbor. By contrast, 45 South's forest-green walls are hung with European oils. A coal-burning fireplace crackles invitingly. Sprays of vanda orchids grace candlelit white linen tablecloths, while tuxedo-clad waiters seem to glide with the background classical music. You want for nothing here.

Among the great appetizers at 45 South is the Cream of Sweet Potato Soup with Smoked Pheasant; any creamier and this subtly flavored soup would be ice cream. I also sampled the Roasted Oysters, but the appetizer to die for is Seared Quail with Brandied Boar Bacon and Peppercorn Cream Sauce. Served over wilted greens, this is a combination you won't soon forget. In order to cleanse your palate before the main course, you are served a light intermezzo of Ginger Pear Sorbet, a delight in itself.

The entrées are just as ambitious. I sampled the Pan-Fried Pompano, accompanied by Sautéed Spinach with Morels. Another excellent entrée is Grilled Lamb Tenderloin with Port Wine—so tender that you hardly need to chew. My dessert was a sinful Chocolate Chambord Pâté.

Before leaving this beautiful restaurant, I went upstairs to take in the live jazz club known as Hannah's East. Those of you who have read *Midnight in the Garden of Good and Evil* will enjoy Emma Kelly,

Dinner

6:00 P.M. until 9:00 P.M.
Monday through Saturday

The Pirates' House serves
lunch and dinner daily;
call (912) 233-5757

For reservations
(suggested)
call (912) 233-1881

"the lady of six thousand songs," and Ben Tucker, a member of the Jazz Hall of Fame. A perfect way to top off a perfect meal!

45 South's Cream of Sweet Potato Soup with Smoked Pheasant

Smoked pheasant

2 teaspoons rendered duck fat   *8 ounces pheasant breast*

Place fat in a hot skillet and sear pheasant skin side down until brown and crisp. Shred meat.

3 medium sweet potatoes,   *2 cups heavy cream*
  peeled and chopped   *dash of ground coriander*
1 small carrot, peeled and chopped   *dash of cinnamon*
1 small onion, peeled and chopped   *kosher salt and white pepper*
1 stalk celery, chopped   *to taste*
2 cups chicken stock

Place potatoes, carrot, onion, celery, and 1 cup chicken stock in a roasting pan and cover with foil. Braise in a 350-degree oven for 45 minutes. Remove from oven and transfer to a large saucepan. Add remaining chicken stock and bring to a rapid boil. Reduce liquid by half. Add cream, coriander, and cinnamon. Simmer 10 minutes, then remove from heat. Purée and strain through a sieve.

To serve, pour over warm pheasant and season with salt and pepper. Serves 4.

45 South's Pan-Fried Pompano

4 ounces olive oil   *kosher salt and fresh*
4 ounces unsalted butter   *black pepper to taste*
4 4-ounce pompano fillets, skinned

Heat olive oil and butter in a skillet until butter turns golden brown. Season fillets with salt and pepper and sauté 45 to 60 seconds per side. Serves 4.

45 South's Sautéed Spinach with Morels

1 ounce dried morel mushrooms,
  rehydrated and julienned
¼ cup minced shallots
¼ cup unsalted butter

12 ounces fresh spinach leaves,
  picked and washed
kosher salt and white pepper
  to taste

Sauté morels and shallots in ¹/₃ of the butter until tender; set aside. In a separate pan, sauté spinach in remaining butter; squeeze out any excess liquid. Combine spinach with morels and shallots and season with salt and pepper. Serves 4.

45 South's Ginger Pear Sorbet

1½ cups pears, peeled and chopped
1¼ cups sugar

1¼ cups white wine
small piece of fresh ginger, peeled

Simmer pears, sugar, and wine in a medium saucepan until pears are tender. Add ginger and remove from heat. Allow to cool; remove ginger. Purée in a blender or food processor, then pour into a metal pan and wrap tightly with 2 layers of foil. Freeze until almost solid; return to food processor and pulse to break up and aerate. Scoop back into pan, cover, and freeze until solid. Serves 8.

City Market Cafe

224 West St. Julian Street
SAVANNAH

As I traveled through Georgia to revise this edition, three people in opposite parts of the state told me to get the recipe for City Market Cafe's Black Bean Soup.

The restaurant sits in the middle of Savannah's restored City Market. The building, over a century old, is a former warehouse that stored carriages and eventually became a feed and seed store before being gutted by fire. Afterward, the area became so dilapidated that by 1959 two blocks of the old market were torn down before preservationists realized what had happened. They quickly put forth the effort and money to save an important piece of Savannah's history.

In the 1980s, the market underwent a complete revitalization, its former warehouses turned into chic shops and restaurants. City Market became *the* place to have a good time, which is exactly what I had the day I visited City Market Cafe for lunch. The menu is metropolitan, featuring owner Matt Maher's indelible signature—like his Black Bean Soup. I also sampled the Stuffed Mushroom Starters. This divine little appetizer combines crabmeat, sausage, artichoke hearts, and creamed spinach and is sprinkled with melted cheese. For lunch, you might try Shrimp Primavera with Pasta, a unique salad of Oriental Grilled Chicken, or a sandwich. Probably the most unusual entrée is Maher's Pizza, which includes black beans, sausage, smoked mozzarella, and fresh tomato salsa.

At dinner, the menu and atmosphere take on a more intimate feeling. This is the time to try Salmon Oscar in Hollandaise, ringed with asparagus and roasted potatoes.

If you have any room left, don't leave without ordering the Choco-

Lunch
11:00 A.M. until 3:30 P.M.
Daily

Dinner
5:30 P.M. until 9:30 P.M.
Monday through Thursday

5:30 P.M. until 10:00 P.M.
Friday and Saturday

5:30 P.M. until 9:00 P.M.
Sunday

Brunch
11:00 A.M. until 3:30 P.M.
Sunday

For reservations
call (912) 236-7133

late Raspberry Torte or the to-die-for White Chocolate Cheesecake. I didn't have any room but devoured them anyway.

City Market Cafe's Black Bean Soup

2 pounds black beans
1½ cups onion, diced fine
2 tablespoons grated garlic
¼ cup olive oil
1 teaspoon ground cumin seed
1 tablespoon oregano
2 bay leaves
1 tablespoon salt
¼ to ½ tablespoon black pepper

pinch of cayenne pepper
1 ham bone
1 gallon chicken stock
¼ cup red bell pepper, diced
¼ cup sherry
¼ cup chopped parsley
1 tablespoon lemon juice
2 to 3 scallions, chopped
2 boiled eggs, crumbled

Soak beans overnight in enough water to cover. Sauté onion and garlic in olive oil. Add drained black beans, seasonings, ham bone, and chicken stock. Simmer until beans are tender; constantly skim top of the soup to remove oil. Cook about 3 hours. During the last 30 minutes, stir in red pepper, sherry, parsley, and lemon juice. Garnish with scallions and eggs. Serves 12 to 16.

City Market Cafe's Chicken and Okra Gumbo

2 tablespoons flour
2 tablespoons vegetable oil
1 cup yellow onion, chopped
⅓ cup green bell pepper, chopped
¼ cup chopped celery,
   leaves included
3 cloves fresh garlic, diced
3 cups chicken broth or stock
1½ cups V-8 juice
1 teaspoon salt
½ teaspoon thyme

2 bay leaves
½ teaspoon cayenne pepper
28-ounce can chopped tomatoes,
   undrained
1 pound fresh okra, cut diagonally
2 cups cooked chicken,
   cut in chunks
2 cups white rice, cooked
3 to 4 scallions, chopped fine
1 loaf French bread (optional)

In a cast-iron skillet, combine flour and oil. Cook over medium heat 20 to 30 minutes, stirring constantly with a wire hand whip until a dark reddish brown roux is formed; do not burn. Remove from heat immediately and stir in onion, green pepper, celery, and garlic until roux stops browning. Transfer to a large pot and add chicken broth and V-8. Bring to a boil. Reduce heat and add remaining ingredients except rice and scallions; simmer covered for 1 hour. Place rice in center of each of 10 soup bowls and spoon gumbo around rice. Garnish with scallions and serve with French bread. Serves 10.

City Market Cafe's Ginger Sesame Chicken

Ginger Sesame Dressing

2 cups vegetable oil
¾ cup rice vinegar
1 tablespoon Dijon mustard
1 tablespoon soy sauce
1 tablespoon fresh garlic, chopped

1 teaspoon sugar
2 tablespoons sesame oil
1 tablespoon fresh cilantro, chopped
1 tablespoon sesame seeds

Combine all ingredients and mix well with a hand whip.

mixed greens for 4 salads
24 steamed snow peas
1 red onion, julienned
1 each red, green, and yellow
   bell pepper, julienned

1 large tomato, chopped
4 grilled chicken breasts, julienned
3 scallions, chopped fine
1 tablespoon sesame seeds

Place greens on each of 4 plates and add snow peas, onion, peppers, and tomato. Lay chicken over top.

To serve, drizzle with Ginger Sesame Dressing and sprinkle with scallions and sesame seeds. Serves 4.

P. Faires

Claudette's Country Kitchen

106 East Central Avenue (Ga. 17)
GUYTON

ollowing the Civil War, Colonel Robert J. Davant, who had served with the Georgia Hussars under General Joseph Wheeler, returned to Guyton and the firm of Davant, Waples and Company, cotton factors. In 1868, Davant commissioned Herman Hirsch, who had been quarter-master in charge of Confederate hospitals, to build a Victorian-style country home with a red tin roof for his family.

6:00 A.M. until 8:00 P.M.
Monday through Saturday

6:00 A.M. until 3:00 P.M.
Sunday

Only large groups
need reservations
call (912) 772-3667

For years after the war, postal rates were expensive and the South suffered shortages of many commodities, like writing paper. But those inventive folks knew how to make scarcities perform double duty. You'll understand this when presented with Claudette's menu, which features a replicated letter on its cover, written in the cross-writing style—from top to bottom and from left to right. People wrote in this pattern to utilize every millimeter of space. The menu letter was written from the Davant house in September 1876 by Nellie Gordon, mother of Juliette Gordon Low, founder of the Girl Scouts. Although the Gordons had taken refuge with the Davants from the yellow fever epidemic in Savannah, the letter describes the deaths of forty-five yellow fever victims in Guyton.

The gigantic magnolia tree and shrubbery surrounding the wrap-around veranda might make you think that this lovingly restored home has always been at this site, but one of its postwar owners had it moved from Main Street to its present location.

Claudette Tuten, who has operated several restaurants in Guyton, says, "I wanted to have a place where people could get together after church, share a meal, and visit with each other. They work all week and don't have time to just talk."

Claudette is famous for her country-style food, which draws people from Hilton Head and Savannah. Each day, the menu is different, because her many regulars eat here every day and don't want a repeat of yesterday's meal. The day that I came for lunch, the cafeteria-style buffet in the kitchen offered country-style Hamburgers with

onions and peppers, skinned Fried Chicken, Pork Chops, fresh Green
Beans, creamy Mashed Potatoes with Gravy, that old-time favorite
Red Rice, Creamed Corn, and a wonderful Squash Casserole.

When I arrived, the smell of bread mingling with the aromas of
vegetables and meats was tough on me, because I knew I'd be visiting another restaurant in a few hours. But I couldn't stop myself
from full helpings of Claudette's delicious entrées and vegetables. I
tried to abstain from desserts but gave in to the luscious, aptly named
Blueberry Yum Yum and the honest-to-goodness Bread Pudding.

Claudette has converted the upstairs into a bed-and-breakfast, so
the next time I wander this way, this will be the place to spend the
night.

Claudette's Country Kitchen's Blueberry Yum Yum

Crust

¾ stick butter
¼ cup granulated sugar

1½ cups graham cracker crumbs

Melt butter with sugar in a saucepan. Remove from heat and add graham cracker crumbs. Stir mixture until combined. Spray a 9-by-12-inch
glass dish with nonstick coating and press mixture evenly around sides and
bottom. Let cool in refrigerator.

Filling

8 ounces cream cheese
1 cup confectioners' sugar

8-ounce container whipped topping
1-pound can blueberry pie filling

Mix cream cheese, sugar, and whipped topping until well blended. Pour
into crust and top with blueberry filling. Serves 10 to 12.

Claudette's Country Kitchen's Squash Casserole

2 eggs, beaten
3 cups crookneck squash,
  cooked and drained
1 tablespoon margarine or butter
10-ounce can cream
  of chicken soup

1 medium mild onion, chopped
2 cups mild American cheese,
  grated
1 tablespoon milk
½ teaspoon salt
2½ cups Ritz crackers, crushed

Preheat oven to 350 degrees and grease a 3-quart casserole dish. Mix all ingredients except ½ cup of the Ritz crackers in a large bowl and spoon into casserole. Sprinkle reserved crackers over top. Bake 30 to 40 minutes until golden brown on top. Serves 8 to 10.

Claudette's Country Kitchen's Red Rice

4 strips bacon
2 medium onions, chopped
2 medium bell peppers, chopped
1-pound can tomatoes

½ tablespoon Tabasco sauce
2 cups cooked rice
salt and pepper to taste
1 to 2 tablespoons Parmesan cheese

In a cast-iron skillet, fry bacon until crisp; remove to a paper towel. Brown onions and peppers in bacon drippings until barely tender. Add tomatoes, Tabasco, rice, crumbled bacon, and salt and pepper and mix thoroughly. Pour into a greased casserole dish and sprinkle with Parmesan. Bake in a preheated 325-degree oven for 30 minutes until rice is dry enough to separate. Serves 6.

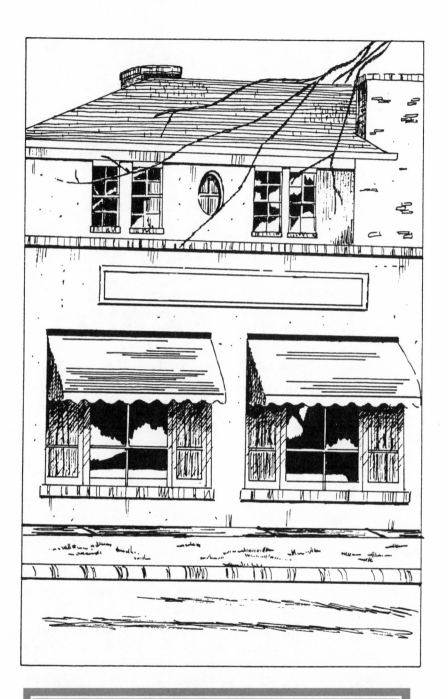

Pansy's of Queensborough

203 Broad Street
LOUISVILLE

The philosophy of Pansy's of Queensborough, as expressed by its owner, is simple. The man on the street wants good food—plain Georgia country cooking. He doesn't want a can of beans dumped out on a plate or a fast-food hamburger, but cooking like Grandma used to do. He wants fresh fish and vegetables, homemade desserts. Not coincidentally, that's just the kind of food served here.

Pansy's of Queensborough is housed in the Old Jefferson Hotel, a stucco structure built in the

Breakfast
6:30 A.M. until 10:00 A.M.
Daily

Buffet Lunch
11:30 A.M. until 2:00 P.M.
Daily

There is a special buffet
every Sunday.

Reservations are not necessary.

For information
call (912) 625-3216

late 1920s to accommodate travelers in the days when much of Georgia's and Florida's trade went up and down U.S. 1. The restaurant starts in a corner of the hotel, where it offers breakfast to all comers in a no-nonsense but cheerful atmosphere of white cotton curtains and red-and-white checkered tablecloths. From there, Pansy's meanders into the hotel proper, which it shares with a local bank. In what used to be the hotel lobby, a hundred people routinely eat a hearty buffet lunch. Beyond the former lobby lies a warren of offices in which the bankers work. It is an agreeable arrangement, since the restaurant regularly feeds the bankers, their clients, and members of local civic clubs. One can borrow money over a plate of Ribs or discuss business under the original tin ceiling.

Sipping coffee at ten in the morning, I was enchanted to see people wandering around eating sandwiches which they had made from a loaf of bread and a plate of leftover breakfast sausages. They would drop a dollar near the cash register and casually help themselves. The man sitting across from me savored one while he told me some of the history of Louisville, and only my excellent upbringing and the fact that he was bigger than I am prevented me from snatching the sandwich out of his hand and devouring it myself.

Pansy's of Queensborough's Fresh Strawberry Pie

1 to 1½ pints fresh strawberries
9-inch piecrust (favorite recipe),
   baked and cooled
¾ cup sugar
¾ cup water

1½ tablespoons cornstarch
2 tablespoons strawberry
   Jell-O mix
whipped topping

Wash and drain strawberries. Cap them and slice the large ones, leaving the small ones whole. Place enough berries in the pie shell to fill the crust, but don't mound them up. Bring sugar, water, and cornstarch to a boil and cook until thickened and clear. Remove mixture from stove and add the Jell-O crystals; stir until dissolved. Pour the hot mixture over the strawberries and refrigerate at least 4 hours before serving. Top each slice with whipped topping if desired. Yields 1 pie.

Pansy's of Queensborough's Pineapple Delight

2 14-ounce cans chunk pineapple
6 tablespoons flour
1 cup sugar

2 cups sharp cheddar cheese, grated
Ritz crackers
1 stick margarine

Drain pineapple. Stir together flour and sugar, then stir in pineapple and cheese. Put mixture into a casserole and crumble crackers over top. Melt the margarine and drizzle it over the crumbs. Bake at 375 degrees for 25 to 30 minutes. This hot fruit makes a perfect accompaniment to baked ham and other baked meats. Serves 8.

Pansy's of Queensborough's Chicken Salad

1 large fryer chicken
5- to 6-pound stewing hen
salt and pepper to taste
1 quart mayonnaise or
   salad dressing

3 eggs, boiled and chopped
1½ cups sweet pickles, chopped
5 celery ribs, chopped fine

Bring fryer and hen to a boil in a large stew pot. Add salt and pepper and cook at a very slow boil until tender. The hen will take longer than the fryer, so remove the fryer when it is tender and let the hen continue cooking about 2 hours until done. Debone the 2 chickens and cut the meat into small pieces with kitchen shears. Do not use a food processor. Mix chicken with remaining ingredients. Adjust salt and pepper. Refrigerate. Serves 8.

La Maison on Telfair

404 Telfair Street
AUGUSTA

In 1854, master builder Jesse Osmond constructed a regal home that borrowed from Greek Revival design. In its 124 years as a private residence, this gable-roofed, three-story buff pink frame home changed families and décor many times. Now, looking more chic than ever, La Maison on Telfair has become one of Augusta's premier French restaurants.

Cascades of tiny white lights frame the restaurant's extended canopy and fill the trees in the back garden. The redone fireplaces in each of the five dining rooms, the antique crystal chandeliers, and the mural-painted walls upstairs lend more elegance than was present when the structure was a residence. The interior walls bloom in burgundy, salmon, and dusty pink. But the real bloom is the creative wizardry of chef and owner Heinz Sowinsky. Born in Mindelheim, Germany, Sowinsky began his apprenticeship at Neue Post Biessenhofen at age fifteen. The school's first rule was never to compromise on flavor. Sowinsky's resourcefulness is what gives him the ability to adapt a dish for a restrictive diet while making it delicious at the same time.

Seafood and game dishes—particularly Emu, Quail, and Wild Boar—provide a tasty and health-conscious alternative to regular fare. But Sowinsky puts a new spin on old-time French favorites by allowing you to choose your own sauce. A favorite of many regulars is his Rack of Lamb Mongolian-Style, but you'll also find an excellent variety of steaks. And though it might look out of place, what German chef wouldn't have Wiener Schnitzel on the menu?

I couldn't decide between the Escargots en Croute with Garlic Butter and the Dungeness Crab, so I took hearty samples of both. After an intermezzo to cleanse the palate, I had the popular new farm-raised fish, Tilapia, which is said to have been the fish used in the time of Christ. Sowinsky grills it and accents it with a fresh, slightly sweet Pineapple Salsa that is perfect for fish dishes and works well

Lunch
11:30 A.M. until 2:00 P.M.
Thursday and Friday

Dinner
6:00 P.M. until 10:30 P.M.
Monday through Saturday

For reservations
(recommended)
call (706) 722-4805

on chicken, too. For dessert, I chose the classic Crème Brûlée, which slipped down like slivers of velvet cream.

La Maison is a restaurant to be savored and sipped slowly like a fine French wine.

La Maison on Telfair's Tilapia with Pineapple Salsa

½ fresh mango, peeled and diced
½ cup fresh pineapple, diced
¼ red bell pepper, diced
2 teaspoons fresh cilantro, chopped
½ jalapeño pepper, chopped fine

juice of 1 small lime
1 ounce rice vinegar
4 6-ounce portions tilapia fish
salt and white pepper or
    jerk seasoning

Combine mango, pineapple, bell pepper, cilantro, jalapeño, lime juice, and vinegar in a stainless steel or glass bowl; cover and refrigerate 3 to 4 hours. Season tilapia with extra lime juice and add salt and pepper or jerk seasoning to taste. Grill to desired doneness and top with a dollop of salsa. Serves 4.

La Maison on Telfair's Dungeness Crab

Vinaigrette

1 hard-boiled egg,
    peeled and diced fine
2 teaspoons mustard
¼ purple onion, diced fine
2 tablespoons capers

2 tablespoons white rice vinegar
2 tablespoon virgin olive oil
salt and cracked black pepper
    to taste

Mix all ingredients in a glass bowl until well combined.

1 pound fresh Dungeness crabmeat
    or lump blue crab
1 seedless cucumber, cut in half,
    then sliced lengthwise

1 teaspoon parsley, diced
1 teaspoon chives, diced
1 teaspoon fresh dill, diced

Stir crabmeat into Vinaigrette; cover and refrigerate 2 hours.

To serve, place 3 slices of cucumber on each of 4 plates to form a triangle;

spoon equal portions of crabmeat onto plates. Sprinkle with parsley, chives, and dill. Serves 4.

La Maison's on Telfair's Escargots En Croute with Garlic Butter

Garlic Butter

2 sticks butter, softened
juice of 1 lemon
2 tablespoons fresh garlic, minced
2 to 3 dashes Tabasco sauce

½ cup parsley, chopped
salt and pepper to taste
parchment paper

Place softened butter, lemon juice, garlic, Tabasco, parsley, and salt and pepper in a food processor and pulse on and off until mixture forms a ball. Remove, mold to desired shape, wrap in parchment, and freeze.

1 medium purple onion, julienned
4 slices prosciutto, julienned
24 escargots, washed several times

3 ounces white wine
French baguette slices

Heat a skillet to medium-high and melt 2 to 3 tablespoons Garlic Butter. Sauté onion until transparent; add prosciutto. Pick snails from shells and add to pan; cook 10 to 20 seconds. Add wine and stir a few seconds more until flavors blend.

Serve with more melted Garlic Butter over toasted French baguettes. Serves 4.

The Partridge Inn

2110 Walton Way
AUGUSTA

$\mathcal{I}$n the late eighteenth century, Governor George Walton, one of the signers of the Declaration of Independence, laid out the village of Summerville. He intended it as a refuge from the summer heat for Augusta's wealthy citizens, but in 1816, when he sold a lot to Connecticut-born Daniel and Elizabeth Meigs, he learned that it also had winter appeal.

Soon afterward, the Meigses built a prominent two-story wooden frame home, which remained in the family until 1861. Around 1900, it was bought by Morris W. Partridge, a New Yorker who had come for the winter as head cashier of the Bon Air Hotel across the street. Partridge turned the home into a small hotel for the "winter people."

People enjoyed coming here for the family atmosphere and the ex-

Lunch
11:00 A.M. until 2:30 P.M.
Daily

Dinner
6:00 P.M. until 9:00 P.M.
Monday through Thursday

6:00 P.M. until 10:00 P.M.
Friday and Saturday

Brunch
11:00 A.M. until 2:30 P.M.
Sunday
On the Veranda

The bar and grill serves meals
6:00 P.M. until 9:00 P.M.
Sunday

For reservations
(recommended)
call (706) 737-8888

ceptional food. The posh country setting became so "in" that Partridge had to build additions five times. The inn eventually grew to five stories, 129 rooms, and a quarter-mile of porches and balconies. Its dining room was hailed throughout Augusta for its excellent cuisine, which food critic Duncan Hines recommended in his reviews.

Today, the inn and restaurant have the feel of being part of an era that most of us only know from the movies. The comfortable lobby seems to say "summer" all year long. And the Morris Partridge Dining Room—with potted palms beside the pillars, forest-green wicker furniture, and lovely floral prints—will make you consider having a mint julep on the veranda before dining.

As soon as I sat down, I received a gigantic, warm Popover with Apple Butter Sauce, which was light and airy. My appetizer of

Shiitake Mushrooms made me wish that Duncan Hines could have had a taste of this popular nineties dish.

People come to this thoughtfully restored inn for many reasons, but mostly because it's truly a Southern experience at its best. The ambiance is gracious without being formal. If I lived in Augusta, Sunday wouldn't be complete without coming here for brunch. You can listen to the music of a white baby grand while filling your plate with seafood and Fried Chicken. Be sure to try the Grilled Salmon with Champagne Dill Sauce. It melts in your mouth and is easily the best I've tasted.

For dessert, I heartily recommend the Crème Brûlée with Raspberry Sauce. Or try the Key Lime Pie with fresh nutmeg shaved on top. Old-time Southerners would probably argue for their Bread Pudding and a cup of cappuccino. It doesn't matter what you order here—you can't go wrong. Duncan Hines would be proud—proud of the food, the way the staff takes care of you, and the inn's listing on the National Register of Historic Places and in Historic Hotels of America.

The Partridge Inn's Popovers with Apple Butter Sauce

Apple Butter Sauce

6 apples	½ teaspoon ground cloves
½ cup apple cider	½ teaspoon allspice
½ cup sugar	1 cup water

Core apples, place them in a large pot, and cover with water. Add remaining ingredients. Simmer for 20 minutes. Blend to a smooth consistency in a food processor or blender. Pour into a jar with a lid and refrigerate. Yields 2 cups.

Popovers

6 eggs	½ teaspoon salt
3 cups milk	2 cups all-purpose flour
2 ounces vegetable oil	

Mix eggs, milk, and oil. Sift salt and flour together and add to egg mixture. In each of 10 to 12 heated, oversize muffin tins, add 1 tablespoon oil and enough batter to fill ²/₃ of tin. Bake in a preheated 400-degree oven for 35 to 40 minutes until golden brown.

Serve with Apple Butter Sauce. Yields 10 to 12 popovers.

The Partridge Inn's Grilled Salmon with Champagne Dill Sauce

Champagne Dill Sauce

1 tablespoon olive oil
2 shallots, chopped fine
2 cloves garlic, chopped fine
1 ounce dry champagne
1 ounce Dijon mustard

1½ cups heavy cream
salt and white pepper to taste
1 tablespoon fresh dill,
* chopped coarse*

Heat oil in a skillet and sauté shallots and garlic until transparent. Deglaze with champagne. Add mustard and bring to a boil. Stir in cream until thick enough to coat a spoon and reduce volume by about half. Strain. Season with salt and pepper and add dill.

olive oil
4 8-ounce salmon fillets,
* skinned and deboned*

salt and white pepper to taste

Brush oil on fillets and add salt and pepper. Grill on medium-high for 4 minutes on each side.

Serve with Champagne Dill Sauce. Serves 4.

Sixth at Watkins, Ltd.

559 Watkins Street
AUGUSTA

$\mathcal{S}$ixth at Watkins is a tale of two sisters. Helen Watson and Michelle Reese joined their entrepreneurial skills to restore this former 1896 warehouse. Floors that once held sundry merchandise to be shipped to foreign ports now hold an interesting array of dining tables with attractive chintz print tablecloths. Neither Helen nor Michelle is quite sure why a warehouse was built with a fireplace, but they've made

Lunch
11:30 A.M. until 2:30 P.M.
Monday through Saturday

Dinner
6:00 P.M. until 10:00 P.M.
Tuesday through Saturday

For reservations
call (706) 722-8877

it into a feature accent that provided a warm welcome the cool January day I came for lunch. Michelle, whose talent lies in decoration, has added a stained-glass window and hung rich Renaissance-style tapestries on the exposed-brick walls, which gives the old building the intimate feel of an upscale club.

Usually, I feel that a dip is a dip is a dip. That changed when I tried fresh strawberries with the restaurant's unique Amaretto Poppy Seed Dip. Be sure to remember this easy-to-make concoction for your next party.

The appetizer I chose was the seductive Shrimp Boursin, which had a slight taste of pepper and bacon. If you aren't a Boursin fan, these mushrooms stuffed with cheese and covered with delicate Chablis Sauce could make you rethink your view.

The restaurant is known for its butter pecan–flavored Muffins, which have a nutty and slightly sweet taste. The trick is to be careful not to fill up on these, because you definitely want to do justice to the entrées.

The hallmark salad at Sixth at Watkins is the Fried Chicken Salad — greens topped with tomatoes, cucumbers, and cheese, with Honey Mustard Dressing drizzled over fried chicken tenders and sprinkled with peanuts. I found that its crunchiness won hands-down over the trendy but also good Marinated Grilled Chicken. I sampled the Chicken Ribier, which is another chicken story altogether. Sautéed in White Wine Cream Sauce and served over fettuccine, this chicken dish has a tender succulence. I also tasted the Seafood Medley, which combines shrimp, scallops, and crabmeat cooked in Lobster Cream Sauce. After a couple of bites, you'll know why lobster thermidor is making a comeback.

The restaurant's signature dessert is its Cream Cheese Brownie, which features vanilla ice cream and chocolate sauce topped with whipped cream and a cherry. But my favorite was the Watkins Special, a pie that uses Bailey's, Kahlúa, and amaretto and is served with five layers of ice cream.

For dinner, the chalkboard menu always features Rack of Lamb, Steaks, Veal, and fresh Seafood. I'm told you can't go wrong if you decide to make your visit for dinner, which many regulars do before taking in an event across the street at the civic center. Or you might have only enough time for a visit to the attractive lounge during happy hour, which is bound to inspire a return engagement.

Sixth at Watkins's Amaretto Poppy Seed Dip

2 cups sour cream
½ cup sugar

3 tablespoons poppy seeds
2 tablespoons amaretto

Combine all ingredients and serve with fresh fruit. Yields over 2 cups.

Sixth at Watkins's Shrimp Boursin

Chablis Sauce

^{1}/4 cup brandy
^{1}/2 cup white wine
1 ounce chopped shallots
^{1}/2 ounce chopped parsley

^{1}/8 teaspoon cracked black pepper
^{1}/2 cup chicken stock or consommé

Put brandy and wine into a saucepan with shallots, parsley, and pepper and bring to a boil. Ignite liquid with a match and allow flame to burn off. Add chicken stock and bring to a boil again; reduce volume by half. Add cream and reduce again by half. Season with salt. Yields about 6 ounces.

Shrimp

2 dozen 31- to 35-count shrimp
2 dozen mushrooms
6 ounces Boursin cheese

4 to 5 tablespoons butter or
vegetable oil
¼ ounce fresh parsley, chopped

Peel, devein, and butterfly shrimp and set aside. Pull stems out of mushrooms; reserve stems for other use. Add enough water to a large saucepan to cover mushroom caps and bring water to a boil; add mushrooms and poach until barely tender. Let cool. Stuff mushrooms with cheese and top each with a shrimp. Butter 4 escargot dishes or muffin tins. Place 6 caps in each dish or tin and broil for 5 to 7 minutes until shrimp are cooked.

To serve, top with Chablis Sauce and sprinkle with parsley. Serves 4 to 6.

Another Thyme Cafe

5 East Public Square
WASHINGTON

he sign reads "Another Thyme Cafe," not "Kitchen Entrance." So I walked right in the back entrance of the cafe's new kitchen. There aren't many restaurant kitchens that are pretty enough to eat in, but you could in this kitchen if tables were set up. Owner Evelyn Bennett says that one reason she decided to relocate across Washington's beautiful old square was that, at her former place, she was tired of cooking under the stairs in a hallway. The roomier setting here seems to have increased the overall quality of the restaurant's food and décor.

Lunch
11:00 A.M. until 2:30 P.M.
Monday through Saturday

Dinner
6:00 P.M. until 9:00 P.M.
Tuesday through Saturday

For reservations
(required for large groups)
call (706) 678-MENU
or (706) 678-1672

This 1895 building served as the old Allen Pharmacy, but it won't remind you of a drugstore. Yet remnants of the past do remain, such as an open elevator. This handy elevator is used to lift tables to the upstairs dining room.

The restaurant's light-colored walls are tastefully filled with huge paintings of fruit and vegetables plus an original 1763 survey map of surrounding counties. Washington is in Wilkes County, one of the original eight Georgia counties. Sherman did not visit here on his famous Georgia tour, but in 1895 a natural disaster conducted a little march of its own through the town square and burned half of it down. The old drugstore is thought to have been built after that disastrous fire.

I sat at an old wooden table in the elevated section near the store-front windows, where I could people-watch. My lunch began with homemade Vegetable Soup. It was chock-full of crunchy green beans, carrots, etc., and I thought about replacing the Cheddar Cheese Soup recipe with the recipe for Vegetable Soup, but I knew the children of my collaborator, Jean Spaugh, would throttle me. Soups and the cafe's many appetizers and entrées are presented with the terrific Swirl Bread—a swirled combination of white and wheat bread made with brown sugar and molasses.

I enjoyed the Sampler Plate, which features a nice, crunchy Chicken

Salad. The thing that puts this salad way ahead of others is tossing the chicken in a meat marinade. The Sampler Plate also displays a tasty marinated combination of English peas, carrots, and pimientos. I sampled bites of the tart and tasty Barbecued Pork Sandwich and a rich, new twist on an old favorite—Another Reuben.

For dessert, I tasted a piece of Fudge Pie, which had the power to make anti-chocolate people (if there are any) into converts.

The next time I visit, I'm coming for dinner so that I can try a Salmon Fillet, a Boston Strip with Peppercorn Sauce, or some lightly breaded Catfish.

Another Thyme Cafe's Chicken Salad

3-pound chicken, cooked in
  chicken stock, skinned,
  and deboned
meat marinade, homemade
  or commercial
2 cups celery, sliced diagonally

1 cup pecan pieces
¾ cup mayonnaise
fresh parsley
tomato slices
hard-boiled egg wedges

Cut chicken into chunks, place in a large bowl, and toss with marinade for a few minutes. Drain marinade. Add celery, pecans, and mayonnaise. Mix thoroughly, cover, and refrigerate. Serve on cold plates garnished with parsley, tomato slices, and egg wedges. Serves 8.

Another Thyme Cafe's Cheddar Cheese Soup

¼ cup celery, diced
¼ cup onions, chopped
1 cup carrots, diced
1 stick butter
½ cup flour
3 cups chicken broth

2 cups milk
1 pound medium cheddar cheese,
  grated
pinch of baking soda
salt and pepper to taste

Sauté celery, onions, and carrots in butter until soft. Add flour and whisk until blended. Gradually add chicken broth, whisking until smooth and thickened. Add milk and simmer, stirring often, until thickened. Add cheese. Mix in baking soda and add salt and pepper. Simmer until cheese melts, but do not boil. Serve hot. Serves 4.

Another Thyme Cafe's Cheesecake

Crust

$^1/_3$ cup light brown sugar
$^1/_3$ cup butter

1 cup flour
$^1/_2$ cup chopped pecans

In a food processor or blender, blend sugar and butter until smooth. Add flour and pecans and blend 2 minutes more, scraping the sides of the processor. Press crust into the bottom of an 8-inch springform pan. Bake at 350 degrees for 10 minutes.

Filling

12 ounces cream cheese
$^1/_2$ cup sugar
3 tablespoons milk

2 tablespoons lemon juice
1 egg
1 teaspoon vanilla

Blend all ingredients in a food processor or blender until smooth, scraping the sides of the processor. Pour into the baked crust and bake 20 to 25 minutes in a 350-degree oven until center is firm. Let cool only about 5 minutes before putting on topping.

Sour Cream Topping

1 cup sour cream
1 teaspoon vanilla extract

$^1/_4$ cup sugar

Blend all ingredients with a spoon and spread topping on cake while it's still warm. Yields 1 cheesecake.

Index

Nutmeg Cream, 1848 House, 37

Praline Tulips, The Abbey, 57

Sherry Trifle, The Olde Pink House, 165

South Georgia Split, Dr. Hatchett's, 118

Pies:

Chocolate Chip Pie, Sassafras Tea Room, 105

Chocolate Orange Pie, The Stovall House, 5

Chocolate Pecan Pie, Rudolph's on Green Street, 21

Fresh Strawberry Pie, Pansy's of Queensborough, 185

Lemon Chess Pie, Sassafras Tea Room, 105

Light Chess Pie with Chocolate and Raspberries, Elizabeth on 37th, 161

Peach Pan Pie, New Perry Hotel and Motel, 109

Rum Chiffon Pie, Seagle's, 146

Entrées

Fowl:

Chicken and Okra Gumbo, City Market Cafe 177

Chicken Duxelle, Oak Tree Victorian Dinner Restaurant, 77

Chicken Fettuccine, The Depot at Covington, 69

Chicken Pontalba, Harry Bissett's, 61

Chicken Tetrazzini, Dr. Hatchett's, 117

Ginger Sesame Chicken, City Market Cafe, 178

Roast Duck with "Shadows of the Teche" Sauce, Rudolph's on Green Street, 21

Stuffed Chicken, The Stovall House, 5

Meats:

Atkins Park Fillet, Atkins Park Restaurant, 54

Dora's Roast Beef, Dr. Hatchett's, 118

Filet du Boeuf Florentine, The Cloister, 157

Grilled Veal Chops with Green Tomato Jus and Crispy Red Onions, The Public House on Roswell Square, 33

Ham and Cheddar Phyllo, The Stovall House, 6

Honey-Roasted Rack of Lamb with Horseradish-Mint Sauce, Glen-Ella Springs Inn, 17

Lamb Chops en Croute, Jekyll Island Club, 149

Pork Tenderloin and Clams Portugaise, The Grand Old House and Tavern, 129

Tournedos of Beef, Beall's 1860, 101

Veal Chop Amaretto, Windsor Hotel, 113

Veal Naturel, Bludau's Goétchius House, 85

Miscellaneous:

Riverfront Gumbo, The Olde Pink House, 165

Southwestern Quesadillas, Atkins Park Restaurant, 53

Seafood:

Baked Grouper, Windsor Hotel, 113

Cashew Shrimp, Seagle's, 145

Champagne Dill Sauce, The
Partridge Inn, 194
Chantilly Cream, Nacoochee
Valley Guest House, 10
Crabmeat Stuffing, Maximillian's,
41
Crabmeat Stuffing, Whitfield's,
137
Cream Sauce, Mrs. Wilkes'
Boarding House, 170
Garlic Butter, Bludau's Goétchius
House, 85
Garlic Butter, La Maison on
Telfair, 190
Ginger Sesame Dressing, City
Market Cafe, 178
Green Tomato Jus, The Public
House on Roswell Square, 33
Hollandaise Sauce, Lickskillet
Farm, 29
Hollandaise Sauce, The
Woodbridge Inn, 25
Horseradish-Mint Sauce, Glen-
Ella Springs Inn, 17
Lamb Jus, Jekyll Island Club, 149
Mandarin Orange Salad Dressing,
The Left Banque, 93
Miso Dressing, The Mansion, 46
Nutmeg Cream, 1848 House, 37
"Shadows of the Teche" Sauce,
Rudolph's on Green Street, 21
Soy Sauce Dressing, The Left
Banque, 93
Sweet and Sour Onion Marma-
lade, Atkins Park Restaurant,
54
Tangy Hollandaise Sauce, Radium
Springs Casino, 121
Vinaigrette, La Maison on Telfair,
189

Soups and Chowders

Apricot Soup, The Abbey, 58
Asparagus Soup, Susina Plantation
Inn, 134
Black Bean Soup, City Market
Cafe, 177
Black-Eyed Pea Soup, Elizabeth
on 37th, 161
Cheddar Cheese Soup, Another
Thyme Cafe, 201
Chicken and Okra Gumbo, City
Market Cafe, 177
Cream of Broccoli Soup, The Left
Banque, 93
Cream of Mushroom Soup,
Maximillian's, 42
Cream of Sweet Potato Soup with
Smoked Pheasant, 45 South,
173
French Brie Soup, The Abbey, 57
Maque Choux, Harry Bissett's, 61
Riverfront Gumbo, The Olde Pink
House, 165
Seafood Gumbo, The King and
Prince, 153
She-Crab Soup, The Olde Pink
House, 166
Southern Corn Chowder, Windsor
Hotel, 114
Swamp Gravy, Tarrer Inn, 125

Vegetables and Side Dishes

Baked Apples, LaPrade's, 13
Broccoli Casserole, New Perry
Hotel and Motel, 110
Cabbage in Cheese Sauce,
LaPrade's, 13
Carrots au Grand Marnier,
Maximillian's, 41
Creamed Corn, The Blue Willow
Inn, 66